By John Fante

FICTION

The Saga of Arturo Bandini:
Wait Until Spring, Bandini (1938, 1983)
The Road to Los Angeles (1985)
Ask the Dust (1939, 1980)
Dreams from Bunker Hill (1982)

Dago Red (1940)
Full of Life (1952, 1988)
The Brotherhood of the Grape (1977, 1988)
The Wine of Youth: Selected Stories of John Fante (1985)
1933 Was a Bad Year (1985)
West of Rome (1986)

LETTERS

John Fante & H. L. Mencken: A Personal Correspondence 1930–1952 (1989)

FANTE/MENCKEN

JOHN FANTE & H.L. MENCKEN
A PERSONAL
CORRESPONDENCE
1930-1952

Edited by Michael Moreau
Consulting Editor Joyce Fante

BLACK SPARROW PRESS ▲ SANTA ROSA ▲ 1989

LIBRARY OF CONGRESS CATALOGING-IN-PUBLICATION DATA

Fante, John, 1909-1983
  John Fante & H. L. Mencken: a personal correspondence 1930-1952 /
edited by Michael Moreau ; consulting editor, Joyce Fante.
     p.   cm.
  Bibliography: p.
  ISBN 0-87685-767-5 : $20.00. — ISBN 0-87685-766-7 (pbk.) :
$11.00. — ISBN 0-87685-768-3 (deluxe) : $30.00
  1. Mencken, H. L. (Henry Louis), 1880-1956—Correspondence.
2. Fante, John, 1909-1983—Correspondence. 3. Authors, American—
20th century—Correspondence. 4. Authorship—Correspondence.
I. Mencken, H. L. (Henry Louis), 1880-1956. II. Moreau, Michael.
III. Title. IV. Title: John Fante and H. L. Mencken.
PS3525.E43Z483   1989
818'.5209—dc20
[B]   89-33428
                                                              CIP

TABLE OF CONTENTS

INTRODUCTION

by

Michael Moreau

Sometime in 1930 a young would-be writer from Colorado wrote to H. L. Mencken at *The American Mercury* in New York expressing a desire to contribute to his journal. Perhaps it was the brashness of youth that prompted 21-year-old John Fante, as yet unpublished, to start right at the top of the literary hierarchy. *The Mercury* was, after, all, the most respected magazine of culture and literature in the country.

What followed was a correspondence lasting more than twenty years, during which time Mencken did publish several of Fante's short stories, but perhaps even more importantly encouraged and guided him along his chosen literary path and often provided sympathetic counsel to the younger man's growing pains, self doubts and aspirations.

When they began exchanging letters Fante was 21 and at the beginning of his career, Mencken, at 50, had worked as a newspaper reporter and editor, had written several books and had edited two magazines. He was arguably the most influential wordsmith in America, and as both a critic and editor he had been a decisive influence in promoting the careers of such writers as Theodore Dreiser, James T. Farrell, James M. Cain, Eugene O'Neill and Sinclair Lewis. For some, publication in *The American Mercury* was the cornerstone of their careers. One of Mencken's young discoveries, Carey McWilliams, was later to become John Fante's closest friend. In his autobiography, *The Education of Carey McWilliams,* McWilliams says of Mencken, "He liked nothing better than to publish a new writer who had something of interest to say about some aspect of American life not previously chronicled. . . . He encouraged me to write about the careers and books of Harold Frederic (*The Damnation of Theron Ware*) [and] about such diverse subjects as religious cults, the folklore of earthquakes, farm labor tensions in California and the life and times of Ambrose Bierce. He also published the first writings of many of my California friends: John Fante, Louis Adamic, Clarkson Crane, William Saroyan, and others. . . . I can attest that he was a prime influence in my 'education.' "[1]

In 1930, John Fante was a student at Long Beach Junior College — inexperienced, but ambitious to become a writer. Mencken, always receptive to aspiring writers, obviously detected an earnestness in the younger man that commanded his attention. In his letters to Mencken, Fante was effusive, bombastic, witty and often plaintive. In one characteristic letter he told Mencken, "I still hold you, and always shall, my ideal of a man, and measure myself by you. I've got to have a god, and you're he." Mencken's letters, in contrast, were generally terse and sober, offering such advice as "Getting a start at writing is a slow business, but if you are persistent you'll succeed." Fante was persistent, and he did succeed both in getting published by Mencken and later in becoming a novelist whose stature now seems steadily to increase.

Mencken, who always took great delight in discovering and nurturing new writers, clearly found intelligence and talent in Fante's outpourings and he encouraged the younger man to write, publishing his first short story, "Altar Boy," in the August, 1932, edition of *The American Mercury,* effectively sending Fante on his way toward a career as a writer.

The letters in this book tell the story of the special relationship between a developing writer and an admired older and wiser editor. Throughout the correspondence, Mencken remains even-tempered while Fante rages against family, fate and the excruciating craft of writing. Mencken responds to Fante's entreaties with extreme patience and straight talk.

The sensible advice Fante received from Mencken, his idol and thirty years his senior, may have taken the place for the younger man of the relationship he longed for and never had with his own father. Judging from his portrayal in a half dozen of Fante's short stories and in the major novels — all highly autobiographical works — Nick Fante, a semiliterate bricklayer from Abruzzi, Italy, was to his son a sometimes lovable, but often a menacing and embarrassing figure. It was a painfully ambivalent relationship which Fante came to final terms with in fiction with the bittersweet novel *Brotherhood of the Grape,* published in 1977. And although the father and son reached a real-life rapprochement in later years, Fante never forgave him for abusing his mother and abandoning the family for another woman in his teen-age years.

When Fante took an early interest in books and writing, Mencken became for him the embodiment of sophistication, the ideal of the writer, his role model. And though much of what he writes to Mencken is thinly veiled flattery designed to curry favor with his editor — and Mencken would have recognized it as such — Fante went so far in trying to emulate the man that for a time he parted his hair in the middle and smoked cigars, Mencken style. Mencken, on the other hand, who never had a son, clearly relished the role of mentor to the several young writers, of whom Fante was one, whose careers he helped develop. For an admirer of both Mencken and Fante it is a privilege to be privy to the exchange and to witness the gradual attainment of self-assurance and maturity on the part of the younger man. It is a long-sustained correspondence, made even more remarkable by the fact that the two men never met.

Born and reaching maturity during the latter half of the 20th Century, I didn't witness Mencken's influence as his time unfolded, but like other apprentices in the writing craft, I was made continually aware of his presence in American letters. One can't think of the Scopes trial without recalling Mencken's assessment of the spectacle, and the national political conventions — before they became predictable and sanitized for television, were circuses defined by Mencken's reporting of them.

Later, working in the newspaper trade, I felt the reverence toward his style and fervor toward the craft of reporting. He remains for many in the profession the standard for incisive journalism.

Early in the 1980s I became interested in the work of John Fante, at that time a greatly underrated writer whose fictionalized accounts of Los Angeles are among the most vivid and moving I had ever read. On first reading *Ask the Dust* I was affected by the intensity of the prose, the colorful depiction of Los Angeles of the 1930s and, most particularly, by the gut-wrenching, funny and sometimes exasperating portrayal of the young Arturo Bandini who strives with finally ambiguous results to master both the attainment of maturity and the skills of the professional writer.

While researching an article about John Fante I met his wife Joyce, who graciously acquainted me with her extensive files on her husband's career, including the marvelous letters that follow. She later told me that her husband never saved anything and didn't like to think about the past, but the Mencken letters were luckily found at the family home in Roseville, California, after his mother's death. Mencken, on the other hand and to the perpetual gratitude of researchers, saved everything. His extensive papers are shepherded by the Enoch Pratt Free Library in Baltimore where Mrs. Averil Kadis, the library's public relations director, kindly assists Mencken scholars in their searches. The actual Mencken/Fante correspondence is on file at the New York Public Library under the Enoch Pratt Library's supervision.

My deepest appreciation is extended to these keepers of the records and always helpful individuals.

The pages that follow form the story of a special relationship between a young writer and a seasoned editor.

The notes leading into the letters and the endnotes at the back of the book are intended to fill in gaps in time and help explain the context of some of the letters in as inobtrusive a fashion as possible, hopefully explaining some of the events and names obscured by time when important to the content of the letters.

I have not altered the text of the letters except to correct the very infrequent misspellings or typographical errors. Little has been done to change punctuation or unusual stylistic usages.

JOHN FANTE & H. L. MENCKEN
A PERSONAL CORRESPONDENCE
1930–1952

In August of 1930 John Fante was 21 years old. He was living in Wilmington, California, with his mother Mary, his sister Josephine, and brothers Tom and Pete. His father Nick had left his mother for another woman, leaving her penniless, and she had moved the family from Boulder, Colorado, to California to be near her brothers. John Fante was trying to support the family with odd jobs on the docks and in fish canneries, jobs that were later depicted in The Road to Los Angeles. *He also took English classes at Long Beach Junior College. In that same August, Mencken, who was 50 and had recently published* Treatise on the Gods, *married Sara Haardt Mencken, a writer and college instructor 20 years his junior. Fante's side of the correspondence during 1930 and 1931 is no longer extant, but there is a clear indication, from Mencken's side, of the relationship developing between the two.*

1

THE AMERICAN MERCURY

730 FIFTH AVENUE

NEW YORK

August 7, 1930

Dear Mr. Fante:

I'll be delighted to see anything you do. I can imagine no reason whatever why you shouldn't make a success of authorship. You write very clearly, and your experiences have given you plenty of material.

Unfortunately, I can't send you The American Mercury, as you propose. There is a rule against it. Worse, I can't offer you pay for Americana,[2] for the same paragraph often comes in from a dozen people. But if you do any writing, I'll certainly be delighted to read it.

Sincerely yours,
H. L. Mencken

2

THE AMERICAN MERCURY

730 FIFTH AVENUE

NEW YORK

May 5, 1931

Dear Mr. Fante:

I am sorry indeed, but at this moment it is impossible for me to take any fiction. Thus I am forced to be returning the enclosed.

My best thanks for the chance to see it.

Sincerely yours,
H. L. Mencken

3

H. L. MENCKEN

704 CATHEDRAL ST.

BALTIMORE

March 27, 1931

Dear Mr. Fante:

Thanks very much for your pleasant note. Who that indignant grocery man may have been I don't know. It surprises me indeed to hear that Baltimoreans are going to Southern California. Hitherto Florida has got most of them.

I hope you don't allow yourself to be discouraged. Getting a start at writing is a slow business, but if you are persistent you'll succeed.

Sincerely yours,
H. L. Mencken

In 1932 Mencken was spending two to three days a week at The Mercury *in New York; the remainder of the week he spent at home in Baltimore, where he wrote a weekly column for* The Sun. *In June and July, he would report on the Democratic and Republican national conventions for the Sun Papers, recollections which would lead to the publication of* Making a President: A Footnote to the Saga of Democracy, *by Knopf later in the year. Fante was receiving mail at Long Beach. His parents had reunited and the family had moved to Roseville, near Sacramento, California.*

4

[1932: undated]

Dear Mr. Mencken,

This person at the typewriter once wrote you some letters from Wilmington, California, last year. I had to. Maybe you'll understand the compulsion when I say that, and it's absolutely true, I was turned from Catholicism and the novitiate a week after I decided to be a priest by reading your *Treatise On The Gods.*[3]

I wrote you. The letter described different mental agonies. I was nineteen, without the gods on my side whom I had got used to, and I floundered about in a sad way. Such floundering is amusing in people past forty, but in me, it was pain. Then your answer came. Courteous and pleasing, it said nothing.

20

A month later you got and returned a story from me. It was a filthy tale. I was ashamed of my mind.

Then I read in "What I Believe" that each morning you saw in your mail that there were worse asses than yourself in the world, and I thought: Well, Mencken, you scummy, hypocritical son of a so-and-so, that's your reaction to my letter, is it? Well, you're a goddam, cheap wordmonger. I was crazy with poverty and worry, I wrote to the man who replaced the God Almighty in my heart, and then he uses my feelings for copy in a paragraph in his credo.

Anyway, what I read taught me blandness. If I'm mistaken about it all, won't you please take my deepest apologies?

Futilely, a man must have a god. You're still mine. Maybe the masochism the Catholics gave me makes me admire you, even after what has transpired. In many ways you're a mighty man.

I'd like you to read the enclosed manuscript. You of all people. It's not great or phenomenal, but it's true to me. I write for a living, though I've never sold in my life. If you buy it, will you send the equivalent by telegraph to John Fante, c/o Helen Purcell, 212 Quincy St., Long Beach. I've asked the same of another editor on another ms., simply because I'm in severe need, practically starving. If it is not worthy of publication, there is return postage, and I will have gotten the happiness of knowing that you read it, which to me is a very great deal.

Thank you, I'm
John Fante

5

THE AMERICAN MERCURY

730 FIFTH AVENUE

NEW YORK

June 20, 1932

Dear Mr. Fante:

For some reason or other this leaves me in doubt, and so I fear I must let it go. Just what is the matter with it I don't know, but it gives me the unmistakable impression of ineffectiveness.

What else have you? I surely hope you let me see whatever you do.

Sincerely yours,
H. L. Mencken

6

THE AMERICAN MERCURY

730 FIFTH AVENUE

NEW YORK

July 8, 1932

Dear Mr. Fante:

After two readings of the enclosed, I come to the conclusion that there is something wrong with it. My belief is that the references to syphilis would shock most readers. The Comstocks can't attack it, but the danger of provoking the Comstocks is nothing compared to the danger of disgusting readers.[4] Thus I fear that I had better let the story go.

May I suggest that you do one dealing with the boy's days in school—his combats with the nuns, and so on? I think you have struck a good vein, and it will pay you to develop it.

Sincerely yours,
H. L. Mencken

7

THE AMERICAN MERCURY

730 FIFTH AVENUE

NEW YORK

July 20th

Dear Mr. Fante:

I am sorry, indeed, to have to report that this piece still seems to me to be less effective than it ought to be. Just what is the matter with it, I don't know, but there can be no question that it somehow misses fire. I suppose the best thing to do with it will be to put it aside for a month and then tackle it again.

I am sorry, indeed, to be making such a report, but that is my best judgment.

Sincerely yours,
H. L. Mencken

8

Dear Mr. Mencken,

Many thanks for your judgment on that last story. I respect it, and I am grateful for it. I suppose one is supposed to get discouraged. I'm not.

The enclosed is a last fling before I take a freight for home.[5] In my estimation it is so perfect that it will be rejected. I mean that I'm not conscious of a single flaw, and that means I have missed again.

Will you answer a question for me? In the past thirty days I have written 150,000 words. I know a writer with a reputation does not do that many, but is a man just starting supposed to do that much? I certainly feel the effects, for, being broke throughout, I ate very little and lost a pound a day, or thirty pounds. I try not to be careless, for I write a thing twice in longhand and finally type it; moreover, to test my immunity to other writers who are often imitated, I read all of Hemingway, Dos Passos, and De Maupassant, besides great stacks of H. G. Wells and a chronic dose of Mencken. This is a lot of reading that ceases to become a pleasure, but a task. It means ten hours of the day and night, including the writing. I'm not bragging here. I just want to know whether a man just beginning to write must necessarily work that hard. I want to know whether you did as much in a similar period of your life. I would like to know from you because you're the only person whom I know whose acumen I respect. I get endless unsolicited advice from people who read a lot and plan to write, but never do it. They give me a pain in the neck.

It is my plan to edit The American Mercury some

day. By forty or thereabouts I think I shall be qualified. This means a lot of hard work, so I am going about it very systematically, and barring death or blindness[6] a man can get whole warehouses of work done in twenty years, and I know no earthly reason why the job should not be mine at the end of that time. It amuses me very much to think that the magazine I shall edit regularly rejects my stuff, nor am I suffering from any delusions of grandness. The only hitch in the plan is that should you ever decide to quit the job, the magazine is liable to go on the rocks, so for God's sake stick around for a while longer. Put your rubbers on and button up your overcoat.

Yours with great admiration,
John Fante
423 Lincoln Street
Roseville, Calif.

I have no more stamps, but they will follow. Many thanks for your generosity in the stamp act.

I saw my story ["The Altar Boy"] in The American Mercury for this August. Pretty hot stuff. My author's note is incorrect. You will inevitably get letters of protest from Denver Jesuits for it. I never did study for the priesthood, nor did I say so in the note I submitted with reference to my past. But I did plan to study at Florissant, Mo., under the Jesuits. That was a temporary vocation which endured for two years. Various things, however, such as skepticism and too much Voltaire and his counterparts, and a sense of injustice over the ruination of my mother's life (too much rel. [religion]) killed the desire for the cloth.

Otherwise, the note is correct.

9

THE AMERICAN MERCURY

730 FIFTH AVENUE

NEW YORK

August 3, 1932

Dear Mr. Fante:

Thanks very much for the chance to see your new story. I like it very much, and am sending it to the printer at once.[7] With your permission, I shall change the title to "Home Sweet Home." The check and proof should reach you in about a week.

I incline to think that you are trying to pile up too many words. Certainly it is absurd to write 150,000 in thirty days. I believe you'll accomplish more if you take things more slowly. If you get one thousand words of good stuff on paper every day you'll be doing well enough. You should have more time for reading, and more for recreation. Very few young authors are able to do actual writing for more than three hours a day. In fact, a good many very successful ones average no more than an hour.

Please send me a new and more accurate author's note. I am sorry about the error in the last one.

Sincerely yours,
H. L. Mencken

During this year Fante was living on and off with Helen Purcell, a music teacher 10 years his senior, with whom he apparently shared Mencken's devotion to Wagner. The first biographical note Mencken received from Fante and printed in the August, 1932, Mercury, *simply stated, "John Fante was born in Denver and was educated at the Catholic school in Boulder and at Regis College, a Jesuit institution, in his native city. He began studies for the priesthood, but discovering no vocation, abandoned them. He is now living in Long Beach, Calif." Contrary to the biographical sketch he sent Mencken in the following letter, Fante was born in 1909, not 1911. His wife, Joyce, believes he misstated his age to make it appear that he had become a published writer even earlier than age 21. The letters below from 1932 focus particularly on the craft of writing and Fante's desire to continue to be published in* The American Mercury. *Mencken's criticism is always constructive and even when he is rejecting a story by Fante, it is the gentlest possible rejection, buffered by encouragement to try another angle on the rejected piece or to submit other ideas. Mencken at one point suggests that Fante should consider moving away from writing about his family, but it was advice Fante heeded in only a handful of short stories. His plans to write a major book about Filipinos in California never came to fruition.*

10

Dear Mr. Mencken,

Ten trillion thanks for your advice concerning working hours and writing output. I respect it absolutely, and I shall follow it. I am very happy that you like the story, and it would be goofy to quibble over the title you have given it. "Home Sweet Home" is all right. The truth is though, that I didn't really sing that song. I can hum the melody, and I know the lyrics, but together, for me they make a cacophonous concatenation, which is eight [sic] syllables, anyhow.

You may do as you please with the following:

I was born in Denver, Colorado, in 1911, in a macaroni factory, which is just the right place for a man of my genealogy to get his first slap, for my people were from the peasantry of Italy. My mother was born in Chicago, so that makes me just as much of an American as is necessary. My father was very happy at my birth. He was so happy that he got drunk and stayed that way for a week. On and off for the last twenty-one years he has continued to celebrate my coming.

I have two younger brothers and a sister. Our family moved to Boulder, Colo., when I was still a little squirt, and I began my schooling there, under the nuns. I returned to Denver for high school, attending Regis College, a Jesuit house. Then I went to the University of Colorado for a year. I quit that place because I was just about to flunk out. I couldn't study there. You see, I'd been four years in a Jesuit boarding school, and you can't imagine the overpowering voluptuousness of everything feminine after four years of confinement. I even fell in love with my English teacher at Colorado, and the hell of it is that she knew it. I made an ass out of myself for real, because I wrote her love letters, unsigned, and she knew their asinine source. One night I thought I'd spill her chastity. I got hold of Sherwood Anderson's "I Want to Know Why,"[8] and I went up to her apartment to find out what the kid in that story was puzzled about. Well, sir, that teacher didn't know what the [kid] was puzzled about. No ma'am, she didn't. But I know, of course. That was [the] Jesuitical technique of making love. I was sure a flop with her, but I'm a lot better today, and I'll go back to see her sometime.

My family went to smithereens a couple of years ago, my father beating it in one direction, and my ma and we kids to California. It was awful. We didn't have a kopek when we got there, and I'm not implying here that we ever had any to spare. I had to go to work. Ye gods, how I hated it. The only work I ever did previous to that was play all sorts of ball. But I got a job, and did a pretty swell job of keeping alive my ma and the kids. I had more than one job, I had twenty-four of them, from hotel clerk to stevedore.

Then my father came back, and the folks went north with him, and I went to Long Beach. I went to the junior college in that town until my money gave out. Money has always been my problem, and the thing I'm trying to do is get enough of it to stop starving. I've done a lot of that, believe me. I'm fundamentally a clever fellow, and I've learned the serenity of honesty. I'm going to do my best to appreciate it the more, but I have a shallow side of me, in the estimate of my friends. I have strong prejudices which I feed. For example, I will not read books written by women or Catholic priests. Though I'm young, I've done a lot of harm. I'm revengeful, and I shall never reach a maximum of tranquility until the injuries and humiliations I've suffered have been compensated. Maybe this is conceited rationalization, but who of human flesh and blood can prove beyond adjectives that I'm right or wrong? Thanks, but I'd rather teach myself, and worship the cherished gods of my own choosing. I have but three, and these'll change soon enough. It's my belief that I can be and do exactly what I want to be and do. Hence, my conviction that I'll edit The American Mercury some day. Yet it's all an elaborately dirty trick, for I might slump over this machine, a corpse, within the next two hours. I have a girl, and I love her, and she loves me, and we both are little pigs for the immense music of Richard Wagner, and so the day is long and good, but tomorrow the sunshine will make me perspire, and the bark of a dog will drive me nuts, and sticky flies will drone and land on my face.

I began to write a year or so ago. Altar Boy, in the August issue, is the only worthwhile piece I've ever done. I have read extensively, and I know contemporary literature pretty well. When Gamaliel Bradford died, it nearly broke my heart. When Lytton Strachey died, I went around all that day with a smile on my face.[9] On Nietzsche's anniversary, which is my Christmas, I always get stewed.[10] I would rather write than anything else.

I have other tastes. I'm a pretty good pug, and I can handle my dukes. I could have been a professional baseball player. My biggest diversion though, and the one which I'll have to give up because it's polluting me, is my *Pimp's Anthology: A Collection of Pornography Gathered From Lavatories and Behind the Barns of the United States.* I have contributors all over the Pacific Coast. I have some swell poetry here, but I'll have to throw it all away. It's a kind of pigsty Americana, and now my collection has so begun to annoy me that I wash my hands with soap and water every time I pick up the book. I think this idea came from my reading of Krafft-Ebing and his pals. I know abnormal psychology thoroughly, too thoroughly for a layman. My ken of the

31

stuff often comes upon me with a rush, nauseating me. This is bad, but it's good schooling. When I was a kid I ate too many walnuts one Christmas. I've never been able to crack one since. So with erotic literature. I can't stand it anymore. I'm fed up.

I want to begin a novel, but I can't, for I must live. My novel will be written though, and it'll be one to make me proud.

Thanks again for all the grand things you have done. I hope I can continue to write things that please you, and above all, I'm grateful for your suggestions as to work hours and output.

With Admiration,
John Fante
423 Lincoln St.
Roseville, Calif

11

THE AMERICAN MERCURY

730 FIFTH AVENUE

NEW YORK

August 17, 1932

Dear Mr. Fante:

    To my great regret, I find myself in such doubts about this piece that I fear I had better not take it. After all, it is impossible for one magazine to take everything. Please don't forget to give me a chance at the next thing you do.

Sincerely yours,
H. L. Mencken

12

August 25, 1932

Dear Mr. Mencken,

    Of all the people in the world, I'd hate to have you think I was a bum, and I mean that to the very utmost.

But this ms. may put me in a bad way in your estimation, so I'm going to tell you another side of it.

My people unfortunately don't seem to get the idea that all I ask is a quiet room and decent mental liberties. They fool with my mail and censor all my books. The latter my mother does. It just happens that no matter what I read it is inevitably dangerous to her religion, and, consequently, I've got to snoop around. There are other books not mentioned in the ms. Gamaliel Bradford's *Bare Souls* I had to hide because the word "soul" was a part of the title. As soon as my mother saw it, she straightway assumed that it was anti-Catholic. Also his book, *Darwin*. My mother nearly fainted when she saw Darwin's picture in the frontispiece. He looks exactly as she suspects a monkey-man to look. There's no use trying to explain that Darwin was a humble, sweet fellow. My mother will not believe it.

And I haven't mentioned that I did all I could around here, even to parting with $115 of the precious $125 for the last piece sold for payment on a grocery bill. My mother remembers, but the rest of them forget easily; nor that they holler about the light bill; nor that the local priest thinks I'm a sinning son-of-a-bitch for writing "Altar Boy," and he doesn't hesitate to tell my sister so; nor that I work under a shingle roof with the temperature at 105 every day; nor that it's no less than agony for me to go to church on Sundays; nor that if I want a good time, I've got to choose my companions. Nor that I stayed home every night but one; nor that these detestable yokels who court my sister hound this house twenty-four hours a day, yelling, honking horns, playing ukes, sprawling all over the porch, and greatly amused because my sister has a brother who writes; nor that I don't knock out their goddam putrid brains, lest I kill somebody. That's all; there's more of the same theme, but it amounts to the same. I hope you don't mind looking at the other side of it. I might as well do the job up right and cut loose with everything.

I have received about seventy-five letters from everywhere about "Altar Boy." I have letters from most of the big publishing houses, from Albert Halper,[11] from Jesuits everywhere, and The American Mercury was a sellout in Long Beach and Boulder, Colo. But there is a letter from Santa Barbara which I think you'll be receiving soon, and please beware of it.

The skunk who will write it is a Filipino named Julio Sal.[12] I used to work with him in the cannery in L.A. harbor. He wrote me at Long Beach, and the letter was forwarded to this place. He wrote that he saw my piece, and that it was a scurrilous insult, and that I was a yellow traitor to the Catholic Church. Sal is a strong Catholic. I wrote him back and told him he was an ignorant boob, and that he was prejudiced because of what happened once at the cannery. Once at the cannery, he was paid by the boss to report any smoking in the building. He caught me and another fellow named Bob Aiken red-handed, and we were almost fired. So after work that night we jumped Sal, threw his clothes in the harbor, and poured stencil ink all over his penis. This was two years ago.

Sal is a man of thirty-eight or forty. He answered my letter, and he writes that unless I apologize for what I wrote to him, he'll write The American Mercury, requesting that my stuff be refused. Well, we shall see. I'm forced to freight out of here, but when I stop in Stockton, I'm going to get one going down the coast to Santa Barbara. If I reach there on time, there's no danger of him writing any letters, since he's waiting now for my answer. He'll get one final answer when I see him. I warn you against him. He's a skunk; worse, he's a fanatic.

I'm not going to fight Julio, but tactics vary with the opponent, and I'm satisfied in the knowing that my stuff is good or bad as it appears in a manuscript, and not because a stool pigeon got what was coming to him.

Mr. Albert Halper is a good fellow and a stout writer.

I'll certainly be happy when I see more of his work in The American Mercury. I still remember the charm of *My Brothers Who,* with Halper's father sitting at the window and pretending not to know Halper was in the room. Halper would make a good substitute for Mr. Charles Angoff[13] when I take over The American Mercury in 1953. I won't forget his encouraging letter to me.

And as you say, "I believe in the reality of progress," for now I have a letter from Albert Halper and many letters on green paper from him who is a better ideal than ten thousand Jesus Christs, twelve thousand popes, ninety thousand St. Johns, ninety-eight thousand St. Teresas, and one hundred and sixty-four thousand, eight hundred and seventy-four St. Josephs; also, sixty-nine million Jesuits and a hundred-and-twenty million Americans.

Which leaves me without any one to pray to for the success of this ms. It's the biggest thing in my life, and I hope it has its merits. And its cash. I can't say where I'll land, but eventually the address on the envelope will reach me, and I it.

Yours for good,
John Fante

I will go to Hollywood to meet Jim Tully, if this sells.[14] I will consider myself able to talk to him, if this sells. Jim Tully is an honest, cynical man who will probably listen if somebody has something to say. He has plenty of muscle, and seems to know the ropes. Like you, he'll listen, whether a man needs a haircut or not.

13

THE AMERICAN MERCURY

730 FIFTH AVENUE

NEW YORK

August 31, 1932

Dear Mr. Fante:

I have a feeling that you had better stop writing about your family. The subject seems to obsess you. The enclosed is good stuff, but I don't think it is as good as "Home Sweet Home," and so I'm not taking it.

Why don't you do some stories about other people? Certainly life in California should suggest a great many ideas. Let me see whatever you do.

I think you should be able to sell the enclosed without difficulty. Widen your markets as much as possible. No one magazine can take all you do.

Sincerely yours,
H. L. Mencken

14

September 23, 1932

Dear Mr. Mencken,

Thanks very much for your kind words with the rejection of my last story. My disappointment at the return was pretty severe for a few days, but I'm seeing now that you are right about the subject matter of those last pieces. I wish I had the capacity for coming to such immediate, accurate judgments myself. It would save me a lot of miserable despair. I learn things clumsily.

I'm writing a story now about a Filipino, a good story, but shocking. Also, now that I'm actually experiencing it, an attempt to be amusing on paper in the shape of a piece called, "How to Go Hungry." I reckon I'll send what I consider the best of the two to you in the hope that you'll read it.

Eleven days ago was a big day for you. Please permit me to offer belated congratulations.

I met Mr. Jim Tully. He said I was too young and too serious and too dramatic and too humorless. I am grateful to The American Mercury for publishing stuff of mine which led the way to a meeting with Mr. Tully. I like him, and he tried to help me.

Gratefully yours,
John Fante

November of 1932 saw the entry of The American Spectator *onto the literary scene. It was edited by George Jean Nathan, Mencken's coeditor on* The Smart Set *and the early* American Mercury, *and by Mencken friends and discoveries Ernest Boyd, Theodore Dreiser, James Branch Cabell and Eugene O'Neill. The opening editorial declared that the magazine had "no policy in the common sense of that word. It advocates no panaceas; it has no axes to grind; it has no private list of taboos." The new venture could only be seen as a challenge to the waning* American Mercury.

In a November 26 letter Mencken wrote to Ezra Pound, "I know nothing whatever about the American Spectator, *and have not seen or heard from Nathan for more than a year. Boyd I see at very long intervals, and then only briefly. The truth is that I seldom read any other magazine. It is labor enough to get through the dreadful manuscripts that pour into The American Mercury office. Far from reducing their numbers, the depression has actually tripled it. Every third American out of a job tries to recoup his fortunes by turning literatus."*[15]

15

H. L. MENCKEN

704 CATHEDRAL ST.

BALTIMORE

November 19, 1932

Dear Mr. Fante:

Thanks very much for "First Sacraments."[16] It seems to me that it is the best thing you have done so far, and I'll be delighted to print it in The American Mercury.

I am sorry to hear that you did not land your other manuscript with Mr. Sedgwick.[17] You probably ruined your chances by appending your hard luck story. Always remember that strange editors are not interested in your personality, but only in your work. If you tell them that you are down with leprosy, or about to be hanged, it only harrows their feelings without helping them in the slightest to do their jobs. Thus they resent it. When you send manuscripts to editors you don't know, say nothing whatever. Simply put your name and address in the upper left hand corner of the first page, insert your stamped and addressed return envelope, and let it go at that.

I'm glad your mother liked your last story ["Home Sweet Home"]. It was a charming piece of work.

Sincerely yours,
H. L. Mencken

16

Dear Mr. Mencken,

Thank you very deeply for your note of acceptance which I have just now finished reading. I can't say too much, and I refuse to be zoomed to the spatial regions by it, for I have found out that inevitably a man can't help himself when he comes tumbling back to earth, so this time I'm going to pretend to be dignified and unmoved about my acceptance, which I am not, nor see any sense in being.

Thank you for your generous words of advice on the subject "The Editor's Reaction to the Hard Luck Story." I think that I suspected all the time that editors feel as you say about such things, but I went ahead and wrote my stupid letter anyway. I am going to be more decent about such a thing hereafter. I can easily imagine a man's reaction, and it's really a lousy trick.

Making a President was "all a wonder and a wild delight,"[18] and I am too happy about it. I thought it was going to lack the characteristic boom-boom, with a lot of crazy little laughs stuck in every page, but everything was there: humor, intelligence, experience, and vigor. I am ashamed that I doubted for even a moment. For despite the ability which comes with maturity of discerning what is not especially true in your books, I can still hold you, and I always shall, my ideal of a man, and measure myself by you. I've got to have a god, and you're he. So, no wonder I am happy when I know that I am going to see my stuff in The American Mercury.

John Fante
(change of address)
c/o Helen Purcell
926 East 4th St., #15
Long Beach, Cal.

17

December 17, 1932

Dear Mr. Mencken,

This is the third version of a twice rejected story.[19] The first time I sent it to you, it came back with the comment that it missed fire somewhere. The second time, you returned it with the same opinion, and the suggestion that I leave it alone for a month and then let you see it again.

This new version is only a third as long as the other versions, but the rhythm is smoother and the story has more speed. I hope you won't be burdened reading it.

Let me wish you Menckens a very happy Christmas. Someone might as well be happy.

Yours with gratitude,
John Fante
(new address)
932 South Lake Street
Los Angeles, California

The rent at the above is paid to January 1, so if you should not get to a report until after Xmas, I'll be grateful if you'll send it to:

John Fante
c/o Helen Purcell
926 East 4th St., #15
Long Beach, California

18

THE AMERICAN MERCURY

730 FIFTH AVENUE

NEW YORK

December 28, 1932

Dear Mr. Fante:

Thanks very much for the chance to see "Big Leaguer." I think you have improved it enormously, and I'll be delighted to print it as it stands. The usual proof and check will reach you in about a week. I shall have them sent to you in care of Miss Purcell.

My best thanks for a good story.

Sincerely yours,
H. L. Mencken

19

H. L. MENCKEN

704 CATHEDRAL ST.

BALTIMORE

January 20, 1933

Dear Mr. Fante:

Don't ask me for assignments. You are on the ground and should be able to dredge up ideas by the thousand. Let me know what interests you, and we'll be able to come to terms.

Sincerely yours,
H. L. Mencken

20

THE AMERICAN MERCURY

730 FIFTH AVENUE

NEW YORK

February 1, 1933

Dear Mr. Fante:

This is excellent stuff, but unfortunately I can't take it at the moment for The American Mercury. I think you should try to extend your markets. Don't let yourself be discouraged if you receive a few rejections. You must be patient if you would make yourself known. Let it go to at least a dozen magazines before you think of retiring it.

Sincerely yours,
H. L. Mencken

please return this letter to me.[20]

In a February 9 letter to his friend, Harry Leon Wilson, editor of Puck *magazine, Mencken's comments reflect on his growing disenchantment with magazine editorship: "Little did I reck when The American Mercury was started how hard it would work me. The Smart Set was easy, for it dealt only with the practitioners of Beautiful Letters, but the Mercury also attracts publicists, sane and insane, and so I linger on a hot spot. For two years now I have been trying to do a book* [Treatise on Right and Wrong, *Knopf, 1934*], *and it is still only half done. Soon or late I must invent some way to get from under this load."*

21

H. L. MENCKEN

704 CATHEDRAL ST.

BALTIMORE

February 7, 1933

Dear Mr. Fante:

Thanks very much for your note. I am naturally delighted to hear that you liked the editorial. I have some doubt that reducing the price of The American Mercury would be a good idea.[21] A number of other magazines have reduced their prices lately, but all of them report that the gains in circulation have been very small. Moreover, there is no desire in this office to have a large circulation. The magazine is aimed at a relatively small group of Americans, and if we tried to interest larger numbers we'd have to compromise with our platform in ways that would often be embarrassing.

Please put your full address on every letter you send out. I spent twenty minutes today trying to find out where to send this answer, and then failed. I must now forward it to New York to be addressed there. It is written in Baltimore.

Sincerely yours,
H. L. Mencken

22

March 23, 1933
Roseville, Cal.

Dear Mr. Mencken,

I thought I'd better write you a letter of thanks. Knopf has gone ahead and let me have about 500 bucks in advance on a novel which I am now working on and will finish in about six months.[22] Of course, what was most instrumental in making this advance possible was your purchasing and publishing my short things. And, too, Mr. Knopf may have consulted you in reference to my synopsis. If he did, it is evident that you thought I was good stuff when it came to writing a novel, because the contract went through in good shape.

Well, to write a man a letter of thanks is a pretty easy and hollow gesture, it seems to me. Everybody does it every day and it turns out to be mere professional courtesy, the same sort that you get from a shoe clerk or a mortician. I wish my gratitude to you were more tangible and emphatic. I don't know how to bring this about unless it be to dedicate my book to you, and, depending on whether or not it is a good book and worthy of the dedication, I shall certainly do it. But I can't tell yet. It is certainly a splendid ambition. Writing a good novel is agony. A big job.

Sincerely yours,
John Fante
423 Lincoln St.
Roseville, Calif.

23

H. L. MENCKEN

704 CATHEDRAL ST.

BALTIMORE

March 28, 1933

Dear Mr. Fante:
If you want to dedicate your book to me I'll certainly be delighted, but I should warn you that I was not

responsible for its acceptance by Mr. Knopf. As a matter of fact, he did not show me the synopsis, and if he had asked my advice about paying the $500 advance I'd have advised him not to do it. That is certainly not because I believe you can't do the book, but simply because I am opposed to advances on principle.

The best of luck to you. Once you get the thing started, you'll find that it will go smoothly enough. I am very eager to see it.

Sincerely yours,
H. L. Mencken

24

THE AMERICAN MERCURY

730 FIFTH AVENUE

NEW YORK

May 22, 1933

Dear Mr. Fante:

It does a man good once in a while to get such stuff as this off his chest, but obviously it could not be printed in a magazine.

What are you up to otherwise?

Sincerely yours,
H. L. Mencken

25

423 Lincoln

Roseville, Calif.

[No date. Follows Mencken's
letter of May 22.]

Dear Mr. Mencken,
Many sincere thanks for rejecting that — er — uh —
"poem." It was far worse than even you thought.

Your question, "What else are you up to?" was
calamitous; the most encouraging question I have heard
in nigh onto thirty-seven years. Here I am, already grey-
ing at the temples, and sweating over a novel which I propose to dedicate to H. L. Mencken. Then . . .

Mannaggia Napole! He writes, What else are you up
to? Swell. Nice work. Perfect. Unprecedented. Shavian.

With your permission I enclose two things: a short
story in the form of a correspondence which I urge you
to reject, and a photographic reprint of yourself which I
got from an issue of Vanity Fair.

Either before or after rejecting the short story, I certainly would be very happy if you'll autograph the print
for me. The picture is a kind of heirloom. It is creased
because I carried it in my pocket for a long time, and it
is badly mounted because the mounting was done by a
drunken school teacher.

Obviously, when God shoveled out the facial
typographies, he had a good time, with many a hearty
laugh, but I know personally that He has done much
worse. I hope you won't consider me a boob for asking for
the autograph, Mr. Mencken. My admiration is not

sentimental, and I say this as Eternal Truth. And I say it with my right hand raised before the image of our Lord and Savior Jesus Christ, "He who wanteth not, nor, like unto the rolling stone, laughs last."

With sincere thanks,
John Fante

Put the autograph on the white border, under the black and grey, and above the word "Americanus."

26

H. L. MENCKEN

704 CATHEDRAL ST.

BALTIMORE

June 5, 1933

Dear Mr. Fante:

I see nothing in this.[23] It seems to me to be very unconvincing stuff. Let it go behind the clock.

I am glad to hear that you are hard at work on your novel. If any of the chapters suggest separate publication, I'll certainly be delighted to get a chance at them for The American Mercury.

Sincerely yours,
H. L. Mencken

In the letter below, Fante refers to "The Odyssey of a Wop," published in the Mercury *in September of 1933.*

27

July 2, 1933
Roseville, Calif.

Dear Mr. Mencken,

This is an old one. I have dressed it up a bit and shorn it of some of the hysteria and tried to add something to it. I think I have succeeded. The original version was sent out five times. The principal kick was its length, so this new version is about a third shorter. I hope you like it. I think there is a big improvement in the writing.

Very sincerely yours,
John Fante

Address:
c/o Max Lieber
545 Fifth Ave., apt 609
N.Y.C.

28

July 14th, 1933

Dear Mr. Mencken,
    This is to acknowledge the receipt of your acceptance
of my story and to thank you sincerely for taking it. The
thrill of publishing in The American Mercury is like
nothing else in life.

Gratefully,
John Fante

John Fante
c/o Jean de Kolty
705 Fay Bldg., 3rd and Hill Sts.,
Los Angeles, Calif.

Mencken left The American Mercury *in 1933. In intellectual
circles the magazine was thought to have become an anachronism.
It was anti-socialist and anti-New Deal. Mencken's editorials ex-
coriated welfare and social reform programs at a time when bread
lines were endemic. Although it had had tremendous influence on
newly emerging magazines like the* New Yorker, *circulation declined
from 77,000 in 1927 to just 23,000 at the time of Mencken's departure in December of 1933.*

29

[October 7, 1933]

Dear Mr. Mencken,

For Christ's sake you *can't* quit The American Mercury! It would be like an automobile without gasoline. I think it's a plain case of desertion, especially at a time like this. The only reason the vast majority of people read The American Mercury is because your book reviews and editorials appear, and without you as its active editor the thing will go to pot within a year or so.

When I read the AP dispatch this morning stating that you were about to resign it was the most disappointing piece of news I think I have in my life come upon.[24] You must be unaware of what The American Mercury means to thousands like myself. I can't understand how you have the GUTS to quit. The fact that the magazine is a possible market for my short stories is insignificant. It stands for a hundred other things. The American Mercury has been my birthplace, my home, my school, my sweetheart, my playground. It has meant life itself. And without you, the American Mercury ceases to be The American Mercury. It becomes the magazine Mencken used to edit. Where's The Smart Set today? In the boneyard. Where will The American Mercury be in a year or so? I wonder!

Oh, Lord. Your resignation has a hundred implications which I feel very keenly. It means you're getting tired. It means you're becoming fed up. The decadence of 1933 begins to stink so you hold your nose and run. The whole goddamn world is hell-bound, and now *you* quit. It saddens me and infuriates me. I think you need a sock in the jaw,

Mencken, the most vital and inspiring man in my life, and now, a mere urchin at fifty-three, he folds up with a bogus senility and decides to quit! Jeeesus Christ. I could almost plead with you. I could almost get sentimental. At the same time I wish there were a law forcing you to stick to your job. I wish some enterprising Americans would toss you in the calaboose for three months.

Whatever way you look at it, your resignation means far more to me than to you, and perhaps I'm more worried about it than any other human being. But that's only natural. Considering the past, it's inevitable.

There's another side to the question, however. I have no doubt that your reasons for resigning are good ones. A man of your qualities never actually deserts the ship, although some one of impulsive judgments like myself may for the moment believe so.

A beautiful future lies ahead. I hope you'll go back to journalism. If your work could get to audiences the size of Lippmann's and Will Rogers' you could do for American journalism what you've done for American literature and American magazines.[25] In two months you could rout the politicians. One man like you is worth ten Roosevelts and twenty thousand popes. It's an honor to dedicate my first novel to you, and I feel I am writing a book worthy of the dedication.

Sincerely yours,
John Fante
207 Fay Bldg.
3rd and Hill
Los Angeles, Calif.

30

H. L. MENCKEN

704 CATHEDRAL ST.

BALTIMORE

October 12, 1933

Dear Mr. Fante:

Please don't take my departure from The American Mercury too seriously. The magazine is still there; Angoff, the managing editor is still there; and Hazlitt, the new editor, knows your work and appreciates it.[26] You'll find your market as good as ever.

I seize the opportunity to thank you for the excellent stuff you wrote in my time. I'll always remember it with the greatest pleasure. Let me hear from you when you feel like it. I hope the book goes well.

Sincerely yours,
H. L. Mencken

31

November 10, 1933
Los Angeles, Calif.

Dear Mr. Mencken,

Now that you have—possibly—more time on your hands, I think it opportune to ask you a number of things which I in my inexperience have not yet been able to answer. I realize of course that 704 Cathedral Street isn't an extension school for ailing young men, but I am very anxious to get my fingers into this new pie, *Advice to Young Men,* which you are said to be concocting.

Most of my thinking these last three years has not really been "thinking" in the sense of a man sitting down and sweating out theories on what he wants and how to get it. What I have done, to be very honest, is imitate you in as much as I possibly could. Temperamentally, I was able to do this; also, I was very poor and dissatisfied; still more, it was the easiest method of reconciling myself with myself. My imitation went beyond mental and conversational gymnastics. It extended to smoking cigars, wearing high shoes, parting my hair in the middle, and staring intently out of one eye at the speaker. For three months I kept a turtle in my backyard, until it bored me and I got rid of it. I used to be vexed because I didn't know what sort of toothpaste you used; and I used to spend hours and hours aping certain Menckenian expressions I came upon in newspapers and magazines. All this was, I realize, more pathetic than stupid, but it represented a period of transition through which I am still passing.

I have discarded the high shoes, but I still smoke an

occasional cigar. And alas, much to my embarrassment, for I think Carey McWilliams suspects me, I still part my hair almost in the middle. But McWilliams has good reasons to suspect me, for I am now in the midst of sending him a bunch of trick letters, a too-obviously Menckenian gesture.

But despite these exterior monkeyshines, I have gained a great deal. I have realized a murky desire to at least be able to say that what I wrote was read in print, and I have, to a certain extent, civilized and oriented a peasant cynicism until it is, at last, beginning to take on the superficial but nevertheless very necessary glow of intelligence. I am not bragging here; I am simply putting down what I feel to be true in my case.

But my progress has stopped here, and I find myelf falling short of my ambitions which I set up and gauge with you as a yardstick. I used to do it chronologically, in this manner: Mencken at twenty-one, a volume of poems; Fante at twenty-one, two stories in The American Mercury. If I still felt the same way, I suppose I could say that I was out-doing H. L. Mencken because he'd never published a novel at twenty-two. But one must be honest and admit he is growing up; besides, I am licked in that I'll never edit the Baltimore Sun at twenty-three. It has been great fun though, and I'm not through yet. . . . I have written the foregoing to truthfully illustrate what your work has meant to me, and to emphasize the significance and faith I shall have in what you might suggest, assuming that you care to do so in response to a difficulty I present in this letter.

It concerns a second book, which I am now contemplating. I want to do it in a deliberately Menckenian manner; [that is to] say, I want to employ a lot of tricks I have picked up from your *Prejudices*.[27] I want to make a lot of noise; so much, indeed, that everybody will hear me. My subject matter, however, is dangerous, and the possibility of being shot down is not too remote. My proposed book, which shall be called *Violent Death,* is going to be an iconoclastic, sociological treatment of Italian Americans. In it, I shall attempt to prove that the Italians in the United States are not only unprincipled murderers but also a stupid gang of lost yokels whose social significance is not in their ability to be good citizens, but bloody clowns: a ludicrous and unsocial people who have forsaken poverty and accepted harlotry.

Naturally, I have a whole slew of preconceptions before I begin this book. I feel that however contemptuous these may be they will eventually do some good, just as the lampooning of Babbitts has done good.[28] But where does one begin, and how do I know that my preconceptions will stand up against statistical research? Or am I to sort my material in such a way as to strengthen the attitude with which I approach the job? In writing this book, do you think it is a good idea to present it exactly in the manner of the *Prejudices?* Or like G. J. Nathan's *Critical Notebooks?*[29] Or, do you suppose it should be cautiously documented and footnoted? Do you think the end justifies the means in that a thoroughly vicious, albeit humorous and intolerant book would eventually do more good than an arid, pedantic treatment such as one might expect in a college? Finally, do you think that, from your knowledge of what I have done in the past, I am experienced enough to write such a book? Or, do you suppose that one who has lived only in the Western part of the United States should leave that subject alone until he has seen everything with his eyes? I know from constant and fruitless searching that there isn't a book on Italian Americans worth a damn, so that whatever I wrote would have to be original; therefore I ask, can one on the Pacific Coast be original enough to cover, on a national scale, some 20 million or so Italian people? Another thing: I can speak but cannot read or write the Italian language, which admits an inadequacy when it comes to the Italian-American press. Do you suppose a reading and writing knowledge of the language is necessary, or will I have to wait until I learn the tongue, which I am now studying?

Here are a lot of questions. Now in a book like one of the *Prejudices* I can get around most of these difficulties by simply ignoring them and writing what pleases me most. I could have a Suite Americano, a great long list of dead gods (saints), all sorts of gruesome murders, essays on Italian writers in this country, on religions, on crooked politics. Indeed, all I'd need as a guide to subject matter would be the table of contents in one of the *Prejudices*. But in the *Prejudices* the material was written around Americans in general, which included Italians. In the book I plan, concentration upon the stupidities of a few ignorant immigrants would offhand seem very unfair. For, on the whole, the Italian people in this country are so poor that very little of the stuff in the *Prejudices* was aimed at them, and naturally it would be a waste of time to write a book about a people who are so uneducated that the vast majority will not even read it. What I want to do more than anything is to so anger these ignorant people that they'll take notice of me first, and then themselves.

I don't think my own intelligence and ability is of great matter in this case because the field is open and I am innately an Italian whom other Italians take immediate dislike to. I feel that I should exploit this capacity I have for making Italians hate me. In this day and age it can't do any harm, because in hating me they will defend themselves, and in defending themselves some of them will use riot guns, but most of them will do a little thinking, which is the important thing.

Sincerely yours,
John Fante
255 Bunker Hill
Alta Vista Apts., No. 23
Los Angeles, Calif.

32

H. L. MENCKEN

704 CATHEDRAL ST.

BALTIMORE

November 14, 1933

Dear Mr. Fante:

Your book sounds interesting indeed, but I certainly hope you don't try to make it an imitation of anything of mine. Imitations always give themselves away. Write it in your own way, whatever that way may happen to be, and put all other books and authors out of your mind. In all probability, you'll have to document it, for if you don't it will lose a great deal of its force and effect. The scheme sounds very interesting. Undoubtedly the book ought to be written, and equally undoubtedly it would, if effectively done, make a sensation. But above all don't try and write it as I would write it, or as anyone else would write it. Do it in your own way.

Sincerely yours,
H. L. Mencken

Fante speaks in letters below about his relationship with his father, Nicholas Fante. Nicholas was a bricklayer born in Abruzzi, Italy. He is depicted in several of Fante's short stories and novels as a rough, hard-drinking, hard-working provider whose sexual dalliances alienated him from wife and family. When John Fante was 19, his father left them for another woman. His mother then left Boulder, Colorado, and moved to Wilmington, California, with her children. The family later reunited in Roseville, California. By 1934, Fante, 25, lived in Los Angeles, but made frequent trips to the family home in Roseville. Although Fante no longer needs Mencken's acceptance as an editor, he still seeks his advice and carefully weighs his mentor's pronouncements, which, pertaining to Fante's love-hate relationship with his father, seem to be quite sensible.

33

1/6/34

Dear Mr. Mencken,

I'm very miserable. There is something I'd like to get off my chest. It's about my father. He used to be a swell guy in my estimation. He used to beat the hell out of me twice a week and I had a lot of respect for the man. There was never a time when he'd come to me for advice and that used to make me sore, but in the last analysis it made me all the prouder of him. Now, he's changed. He's through. It tears out my guts when I think of it. You see, my old man wanted to be a singer when he was a kid, but he was poor, and didn't get a chance. He had to work like a dog from the age of twelve, and it embittered his whole life. It made a brute out of him in many ways.

The last time I saw him it nearly killed me. All his fire is gone. He's only fifty-three, but this worrying through the depression has taken a deep cut out of his vitality. He's like a goddamn kid again. He goes around puffing a cigar and bragging about me. Christ. I hate it. He was never that way. He was *always* right, and that's why I loved him. But now he's changed. When I was home, he was out front fixing the lawn mower. I was sitting on the steps watching him. He couldn't get it fixed. He called me over, and he asked, "Can you see what's wrong with it?"

My old man will never realize it, but he killed me when he said that. I nearly fainted. I damned near started to cry. He *shouldn't* have asked me for advice. The goddamned fool! He should have bluffed it.

Then something else:

I had some new shirts in my grip, and he wanted one of them. I told him to go ahead and help himself. But the fool! The goddamned ignorant blind fool insisted that *I* pick out the shirt for him. This thing is nearly killing me. I can't sleep thinking about this man who is my father and is growing old. He doesn't know it, the old bastard, but I'd love him a thousand times more if he'd continue to think I was the worst fool on earth, instead of one of the coming men in literature.

He sits on the porch with a Mercury in his hands, reading my stories. All day long. The son of a bitch! He holds it up close because his eyes aren't what they used to be, and he squints at it, and reads slowly, slowly, slowly. The man never did read until a year ago. Oh, shit! Every once in a while he chuckles. He goes around town asking people if they know who *Johnnie* is. What am I going to do? He carries a list of my published stories. He brags and brags. I break down and cry like a child when I think of it. Why does he have to do that? Why can't he continue to be my father? Why do I have to be the pace-setter? Why can't he be a man and stand up and say his son is a fucking low-down bastardly fool, which would be true? He puts footnotes to my mother's letters, and they read, "Write to your Papa. He wants to here from you." And he signs it with a magnificent flourish: NICK FANTE. Oh, hell. He would never, never, never understand how I feel. The old fool is even changing his habits. He's laying off hard liquor. He's staying home nights. He goes to mass on Sundays. Goddamnit Mencken, you don't know how I feel. You can't believe the respect and love I had for that man, and I thought he was great, and now look at him, a fucking mass-goer.

I used to love to hear the guy swear, and he could swear like a trouper. He used to get into brawls and come home with a black eye and a torn shirt, but now it's all over. He's quit everything. He's ceased to exist. He worries about me; overtly, I mean. In the papers he read about the earthquake,[30] and didn't go to sleep that night. Three years ago he would have gone to sleep. Three years ago he would have carried on like a man. New Year's Day he sends me a telegram because of the flood. "Are you alright? Let us know." And I all the time in bed with a female, both of us stinko from Planters Punch! What hurts and hurts is that he's getting helpless without me. It isn't that I don't love him, because my pity is ten thousand times stronger than my love. But why can't he fake it? After all, I'm only a punk kid myself. Why can't he wait another ten years? Why give me the responsibility of his idealization and expectations? I can't bear it. I am too aware of my limitations. I am not in the slightest what he thinks I am. I *can't* expect to be. To have a father fawning at a man when he's only twenty-two is too much. It breaks everything down.

So every old man I meet on the streets is my father.

Every old man twists my guts with an uncontrollable pity that leaves me helpless. I want to take the old galoots in my arms and pat them on the back and tell them to quit their kidding, that they're mere kids, and that the world is still in terror of them. At the same time I wish each and every one of them were dead, because it seems to me only a few men ever achieve the fine art of growing old.

This has probably been very boring to you Mr. Mencken. I felt though, that I had better get the thing out of my system. It has been pestering me for months. There are few men who understand what I've tried to put down here. They're all too ready to say I'm stupid, or that I'm sentimental, and afraid to face the facts. Hell! I'm not afraid of anything. A thing like this leaves me cold, though. I am very sensitive to it. About the only thing one can do is tell somebody else, and at this time I'm too unhappy to try to make a story out of it, though some day I will.

Confidentially,
John Fante
255 So. Bunker Hill #23
Los Angeles

34

H. L. MENCKEN

704 CATHEDRAL ST.

BALTIMORE

January 13, 1934

Dear Mr. Fante:

I see no reason why you should be upset about your father. What you are facing is simply the ancient fact that as men grow older they lose their assurance and turn increasingly to the young. If the two of you live long enough you will find your father deferring to you as if you were Socrates. Meanwhile, he needs your sympathy. He is quite as well aware of the change that has overtaken him as you are, and it probably distresses him considerably in his private moments. The way to buck him up is to defer to him as much as possible.

Sincerely yours,
H. L. Mencken

35

January 25, 1934
Los Angeles, Cal.

Dear Mr. Mencken,

Thanks awfully for your generous and wise advice about my father. It had never occurred to me that the difficulty was as obvious and as simple as you suggested. The trouble had me by the ears, as in an obsession. I was exaggerating its aspects.

After receiving your letter, I wrote my old man. As best as I can remember, it was either the second or third letter I have ever written him in my life, since in writing home I always address my mother. He answered immediately; indeed, by air mail, and what he had to say is proof for his delight and faith. It was an astonishing letter, and I got a great wallop out of it. In fact, I was skeptical of its origin, and would not have believed it but for the familiar handwriting.

Why don't you start a harem? You've got something on the ball that all women wail about. Particularly among school teachers. I have yet to meet a school teacher who does not titter and blush when your name is mentioned. In my own modest circle, you are something of a rival. Your latest intrusion happens to be between myself and a music teacher in a local high school.[31] If I may be so vain as to say so, this lady has always congratulated me on my cocksmanship, and I have some poetry to prove it, to say nothing of a drawer full of testimonial letters.

Recently, she has begun to show an irksome curiosity about H. L. Mencken, for I have mentioned your work to her a good many times. As I said before, this woman is a music teacher, and all a man need do to make her an enemy for life is to discuss flippantly any phase of good music. Generally, she is a gentle person, about thirty-four, and very refined. But in the course of an evening if one should turn the radio dial to a jazz program, she curses in the most obscene language I've ever heard. At first I thought this was an affectation, but now I know she's terribly sincere in her outbursts. She despises jazz.

Not long ago, she began to compose what she called a symphonette to me, since, if I may be so ruthless in saying it, I'm undoubtedly her one true love — depending entirely on how she feels. About the same time that she began the composition in praise of my bedding talents, she began to read at random from your many *Prejudices*. Therein she found all sorts of dabs and dissertations on music, *her* kind of music. She went completely nuts. You can imagine my depression when, last night, she told me that the symphonette in my honor had caused her no end of trouble, and that she had decided to abandon it. My natural modesty forbade me coaxing her to continue the composition, and for the rest of the evening I had to be content with common verbal flattery. Even this was very lackluster, and I got suspicious. All at once she clasped her hands to her breast and let the following go (ordinarily she speaks straightforward unpretentious English): "Ah, that Papa Mencken! He ees wan' gran' fallo!"

Well, Jesus Christ! Then she said, "He loffs Schubert like I loff heem!"

I retreated to the piano bench, and there before my eyes on the music stand was the unfinished score of the symphonette. Though I can't read music, I saw from eraser marks that the work had been through considerable tempering. The dedication at the top (my name) had been done away with, and there was nothing written in its place. It looked very obvious to me, and, to paraphrase Hemingway in more ways than one, "I didn't say anything."

Sincerely,
John Fante
255 So. Bunker Hill
Los Angeles, Calif.

36

H. L. MENCKEN

704 CATHEDRAL ST.

BALTIMORE

February 6, 1934

Dear Mr. Fante:

You and your father are going through a difficulty that afflicts all fathers and sons. It will pass off presently, and you'll be on better terms with him than ever before.

Tell the musical lady that I have long since retired from general practice, and that even my son Julius is talking of settling down.[32]

I am sailing on Saturday for the Mediterranean, and

hope to make a brief visit to the country of your ancestors. After that I'll proceed to Jerusalem and view the relics of the Holy Faith.

Sincerely yours,
H. L. Mencken

Mencken and his wife, Sara, departed in mid-February for a two-month Mediterranean cruise.

Fante, who persists in misstating his age — he is actually 25 — sends Mencken a copy of the manuscript of Pater Doloroso, *the novel he was under contract for with Alfred A. Knopf, which the publisher rejected.*

37

Venice, Cal.
4/8/34

Dear Mr. Mencken,

Welcome home, you tramp. When you left The American Mercury it was bad enough. Leaving your native land was a crime against patriotism. God knows how we got along without you. I personally put down six revolutions. Had you stayed in Europe another week every building in America would have been razed and Wirts would have been at the helm.

Anyhow, I'm celebrating my twenty-third birthday by mailing my novel and welcoming you back. I had a feeling you would go to the Orient and return via one of the transpacific seaways. Then you could have spent a few days in Los Angeles. Had you done so, we could have gone whaling. This is whale season, you know.

The book is a flop. It fell to pieces when I tried to remove the super-structure. I wrote a million words, and four drafts. Out of it I got a 220-page hodge-podge. And it's all old stuff, an elaboration of that stuff in the Mercury. If you read it, please remember that I was writing within the limitations of a synopsis bought and paid for under contract. Incidentally, I understand now why you are against advance royalties on a book. Both parties suffer. There is no slobbering in the dedication. It is simply, "For H. L. Mencken and Ross B. Wills," the latter a friend.

Dedicating books to you is right up my alley, Mr. Mencken. My next book will be a colossal affair. I have already begun taking notes on it. It is going to be a modern Huckleberry Finn. Assuming that I don't have to worry about money, I'll get it finished by Christmas, I'm chafing to read your book on morals, and my name is first on the library's reserve list. I hope to God it's as good as the last 75 pages of your *Treatise on the Gods*. I guess you yourself know that those pages were the greatest streak of sheer writing and thinking in all your works.[33]

In conclusion I say again that I'm delighted to know you're back again.

Most sincerely,
J. Fante
c/o Carey McWilliams
900 Spring Arcade Bldg.,
Los Angeles, Calif.

71

38

H. L. MENCKEN

704 CATHEDRAL ST.

BALTIMORE

April 17, 1934

Dear Mr. Fante:

You are going through the agonies that every young author must face. It is a burden laid by God upon those who presume to invade his prerogatives. It would probably be good for you to throw the manuscript away altogether and start upon another. There is a great deal of wastage in the literary business, particularly in its early stages.

Your letter is somewhat vague and I can't gather whether the manuscript is heading for me or for the publisher. If it is coming to me I'll naturally read it at once, and with the greatest pleasure.

Sincerely yours,
H. L. Mencken

Fante's letters below deal with his apprencticeship in Hollywood. It was his friend Carey McWilliams who first introduced him to Ross Wills, the head script reader at MGM. Wills, Fante and McWilliams became drinking buddies, often meeting at Musso and Frank's, the Hollywood writers watering spot. But, most significantly, it is the beginning of the Hollywood period of Fante's writing career — the work as a scenarist and screenwriter toward which Fante feels considerable ambivalence as attested to by the dialogue with Mencken in many of the following letters.

In an unpublished interview in 1977 with an Argentinian filmmaker, Einar Moos, Fante summarized his early years in films: "The first opportunity came when I worked in collaboration with a writer by the name of Frank Fenton. We wrote an original story and sold it to Warner Brothers. And they needed someone to write the screenplay, and they selected me because they felt that I was more professional since I had published stories in magazines. So, I got my first job at Warners and there I was for ten or twelve weeks and when that job ended, I went back to my apartment with the intention of writing another book. I got an offer from Warner Brothers for the second time and I was there for quite a long period — four or five months, or something like that. And from there, I went to RKO and then, subsequently I worked for Paramount, and then I worked for Orson Welles, RKO, MGM, Republic — almost all the studios. Columbia. So, I had a taste of every studio in town" About the work, he said, "I didn't care too much for the assignments or the work as compared to a novel. I found it too compromising."

Besides the compromising quality of the work, the letters also indicate Fante's disdain for some of the doctrinaire leftists he encountered both at a San Francisco writers conference and in his film writing career. Like Mencken, Fante was (as his wife, Joyce, recalls) skeptical of politics, and politics pervaded Hollywood in the 1930s.

39

Culver City
June 16, 1934

Dear Mr. Mencken,

In these treacherous days I fortify myself with heavy doses of Nietzsche who, for all his little errors, is the best medicine in the world. It takes a terrific amount of it to write the stuff I'm now writing, and still go on living from day to day. The hell of it is, I'm writing for the studios, and it's the most disgusting job in Christ's kingdom. Once long ago I thought it would be great fun to do a scenario, but I have had a shocking reversal of that theory. So I work hard all day, and read Nietzsche all night.

I wouldn't be scribbling this motion picture slop except that I've had very bad luck in the past three months, and that a scenario writer makes fifty times as much money as James Branch Cabell and Sherwood Anderson[34] put together. My work is in collaboration with a man who has a potent entree to the Selznick[35] office; so potent, indeed, that this scenario we're doing, though based on the career of the murderer Dillinger, is liable to go through. The whole thing is a nasty piece of hypocrisy: the triumph of good over evil. My partner and I have forced John Dillinger and his pals into Death Valley, California, and little by little the Lord is killing them off. The fiends die one by one of rattlesnake bites, lizard bites, tarantula bites, poison water, and hunger. It's all very terrible, and only goes to show what happens to sinners who break the law. Despite the obscene wails of the stinking, rotting modern Catholic church in the papers every day, we may swing this picture. If so, I shall put my money in a suitcase and flee to the hills, where I can write my novels in comfort. (I know you don't believe a word of it.)

This famous first novel of mine, which I have been boasting about for the last thirteen months, was really a pretty lousy novel. Mr. Knopf was bitterly disappointed in it and insists that I go to work on another one to satisfy the demands of the contract. I could have pushed matters and insisted that Knopf abide by the contract and publish the book, but that would have been very foolish. I am not as anxious to get into print as I used to be, and I am honestly glad for the opportunity to try again. The book was truly a bad novel, and no one would have got any good out of its publication.

I think I shall soon be back in the Mercury again. Mr. Angoff has asked me for some stuff, and I sent him a pretty good short story on the recent Long Beach earthquake. He liked it with the exception of one bad spot, which he asked me to rewrite. This I have done.

A month ago my agent Maxim Lieber turned down a story of mine because it was ironically pro-Catholic.[36] The truth is, I was not aware of any bias when I wrote the yarn. The whole story came easily and naturally to me. The writing was pretty good. Lieber said so. Fact is, he said it was a good story and that undoubtedly I would be able to sell it. I am still burning up at the thought of an agent, a mere agent, a goddamn Marxist, a goddamn dabbler in Marxism, rejecting a story because it displeased his current whim. This is the third time it has happened to me. Certainly *you* wouldn't have done that; I recall a lot of things you published which were not in harmony with your principles. A story is a story; if it's good, it should be printed. But because a story happens to be Catholic in theme there is no reason why a fucking goddamn agent — who's supposed to handle literary work and not propaganda — should turn it down. I am finished with that man; moreover, I'm going to get him at the first opportunity.

What do I care for Communism? They can put me against the wall and shoot me before I'll subscribe to the parlor Marxism of a stupid gang of Harvard graduates who — because they have nothing in their hearts — must swallow and defend principles they know nothing about. Today, every bohemian and lesbian and fairy is a Communist. I am sick of them! And before they keep me out [of] print they'll have to tear me to pieces. They are ten times as bad as Babbitts. They "sympathize" with the masses. That's a lie. They use the masses for copy, but they do not sympathize except hypocritically. Look at Dreiser and Anderson. Those men aren't Communists in sincerity. They are Communists because Communism pays in this country. I personally have no sympathy with the masses. The masses will always exist. They are fools. They are necessary to society. If anything, I hate the masses. I have lived with them, and I have smelled their dirty breaths and bleak minds. Education will not touch them. Nothing can touch them. They are doomed. Let them die. My business in life is to save myself. That's a tremendous job. I shall not dirty my hands trying to save the masses.

But the question is, are there any honest agents in New York City? If you know one, and care to recommend him, he could be very useful to me. As so often happens, I don't have the postage to send my stuff to the various possible markets.

The *Treatise on Right and Wrong* was worth its price a hundred times. I see the pedagogues are attacking it, which is a good sign, and I was much amused by the review of that cross-eyed writer in the New Masses, whoever he was.[37] I hope the book enjoys the large sale it deserves.

Sincerely,
J. Fante
2316 Clyde Avenue
Los Angeles, Calif.

40

H. L. MENCKEN

704 CATHEDRAL ST.

BALTIMORE

June 29, 1934

Dear Mr. Fante:

I find your letter of June 16 on my return to Baltimore. So far as I know, Lieber is the best agent in New York. If he fails, then all the rest are likely to fail. My opinion, as you know, is that agents in most cases are unnecessary, but I usually recommend them to authors living at a considerable distance from New York.

It is too bad that you couldn't come to terms with Knopf. But inasmuch as you agree with him that the novel was probably not what it should have been, I suppose there is nothing to be done about it. I always advise young authors to scrap their first two or three book manuscripts. Many a man has been ruined by being published prematurely. After you have done two novels you'll be able to make a third that will be ten times better than either.

The movie enterprise sounds excellent. I see no reason whatever why you shouldn't get something from the movie magnates in order to finance the work you want to do.

Sincerely yours,
H. L. Mencken

41

July 12, 1934
John Fante

Dear Mr. Mencken,

Thanks ever so much for your last little letter. Receiving one from you continues to be the best pleasure I know about. Sometimes though I wonder whether or not you consider my correspondence a nuisance and a bore. Often enough I have to invent excuses for writing you; I suppose you suspect as much. Do you mind? I know you are a very busy man with enough troubles of your own, and I gauge my letters accordingly. I often feel like writing you at great length, but there is hardly anything to tell you that you don't already know about, and thus I am stopped cold.

You see by now what has happened since you retired from the editorship of The American Mercury. Once more the country is infested with literary and political quacks who have been hibernating for ten years. I may be stupidly prejudiced, but my conviction is that never in my life have I seen a greater exhibition of imbecilities and frauds than at this moment. All over the land the mob is roaring for blood, the politicians are resorting to their basest tricks, and organized religion is showing the intrinsic gutlessness of its tenets. The strikers are being slaughtered and canonized as fast as the National Guard shoots them down; in San Francisco the Longshoremen consider it a blue day unless one of their stooges is slaughtered by the yellow-bellied militia; God and a somber-jawed thief takes his place: both come from the same incubator, and the difference is one of countenance rather than principle.

Meanwhile schoolteachers and literary hostesses and smelly slovenly radicals await the New Day of Upton Sinclair. By the time he settles his opportunistic can in the governor's seat, the Democrats will have castrated him and locked him in the capital building and hidden the key. All the respect I had for that man left when he threw his hat in the California pig-pen and announced that he would save the state. Laughing at him is futile. His is a pathetic finish for a man who has in the past been so inspiring. The last straw would be a newspaper notice of the fact that H. L. Mencken is running for the governorship of Maryland. I would take poison or finish like Nietzsche.[38]

With a whole nation plunging toward destruction because of crooked politicians, the clergy suddenly comes to the fore and howls for purity in motion pictures. Every day the papers publish the speeches of well-fed cardinals and archbishops, giving them fifty times more column space than they deserve.[39] Meanwhile the fact that honest men are dying of hunger is no longer even printed. The whole miserable drama is too disgusting to watch. I find it impossible to enjoy and the longer I observe it the sharper my acumen, the sadder my heart, for even as you and I, those in the spectacle are human beings, members of the same race and nation, products of the same institutions. Leaving the country would not change matters. The show is lousy in no matter what theatre.

I am feeling more and more a desire for organization, simply in self-preservation. The force of events is driving the men of my age in this country, and exerting pressure: proceeding with plenty of guns and rope and exterminating the monsters who were our fathers and pioneers. But that is a part of myself I cannot give, and in the second place nine out of ten of my contemporaries have already been perverted by American Democracy and will very shortly shed their blood for another war slogan. I am not afraid. I shall do exactly as you did during the last war.[40] So long

79

as I have an intellectual ideal apart from my own emotion I can act like a civilized man and go the whole hog. I might weep a little and sentimentalize the whole business but I shall always be able to say that it was my thought and not my flesh that made me hang on. In this place permit me to make a suggestion for your book on young men. There should be a chapter entitled "What to do in Time of War." You could really go to town on that one. Another should be, "How to Read a Newspaper."

You were correct about the idea of writing at least three novels before publishing one. Indeed, I am so convinced of the truth of what you say that I am tempering my regular output considerably and writing with the idea that, after all, there is no need to hurry the job. Maugham writes two novels a year, but nobody remembers anything but *Human Bondage*. Sinclair Lewis could have quit after *Main Street,* and Anderson after *Winesburg, Ohio,* and so on.

Very sincerely,
J. Fante
2316 Clyde Avenue
Los Angeles, Calif.

H. L. Mencken with copies of *The American Mercury* on
his desk, 1928. *Photo courtesy Enoch Pratt Free Library.*

Sara Mencken and H. L. Mencken, September 4, 1930.

John Fante, working as a busboy at Marcus' Grille in
Los Angeles, 1933. *Los Angeles Herald Express* photo.

H. L. Mencken, 1933. Photo by Ray Jackson. *Photo courtesy Enoch Pratt Free Library.*

H. L. Mencken, 1935. *Photo courtesy Enoch Pratt Free Library.*

H. L. Mencken, 1936. *Photo courtesy Enoch Pratt Free Library*.

H. L. Mencken, February 21, 1936.

Joyce and John Fante, 1937.

John Fante, circa 1938.

John Fante, 1938.

Joyce and John Fante at Ciro's restaurant in Hollywood,
1939.

John Fante in San Francisco, circa 1940.

H. L. Mencken, 1941.

H. L. Mencken, circa 1942. *Photo courtesy Enoch Pratt Free Library*.

H. L. Mencken, 1942. *Photo courtesy Enoch Pratt Free Library.*

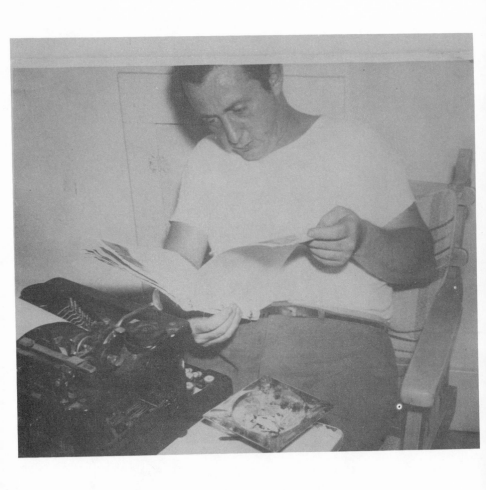

John Fante in Roseville, 1943.

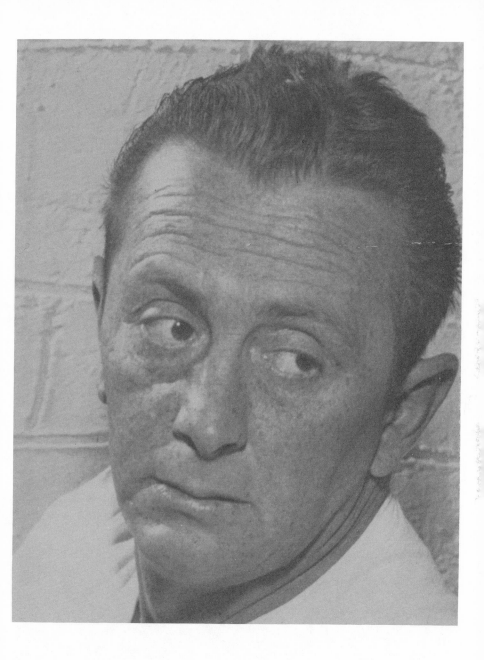

John Fante, 1944.

John Fante's parents, Nick and Mary, circa 1945.

Hal Boyle, AP columnist, and H. L. Mencken, 1947.
Mencken is quoted as saying "another war is inevitable."

John Fante, circa 1948.

John Fante at home in Malibu, 1951.

William Saroyan, John Fante, Mrs. Carol Saroyan and Mrs. Hayes Goetz, 1952. On March 6th, Mrs. Carol Saroyan was granted an interlocutory decree of divorce from novelist William Saroyan after a 20-minute hearing in Santa Monica Superior Court. John Fante was a witness for William Saroyan and Mrs. Hayes Goetz for Carol Saroyan.

42

H. L. MENCKEN

704 CATHEDRAL ST.

BALTIMORE

July 17, 1934

Dear Mr. Fante:

There will certainly be a chapter in *Advice to Young Men* on what to do in time of war — in fact, I have more notes for it than for any other chapter. The subject has been horribly obscured by rogues and sentimentalists.

The over-production of quacks that you notice [is] always visible in times of public difficulties. The American people are firmly convinced that every imaginable disease is curable, and when the regular doctors fail to relieve them they turn at once to quacks. My belief is that all of the members of the Brain Trust belong to this category. I can see nothing whatever in them save the desire to line up at the public trough — in brief, they are jobholders precisely like any others. The notion that they are altruists is sheer insanity, and the notion that they are master minds is almost as crazy.[41]

Sincerely yours,
H. L. Mencken

In the letter below, Fante makes reference to Mencken's publishing the following stories in The American Mercury: *"Altar Boy," August, 1932; "Home Sweet Home," November, 1932; "First Communion," March, 1933; "Big Leaguer," March, 1933; and "Odyssey of a Wop," September, 1933. He also refers to the publication of "One of Us" in* The Atlantic Monthly, *October, 1934.*

43

July 29, 1934
John Fante

Dear Mr. Mencken,

Thanks to you and your wonderful kindness in publishing me in your Mercury days, the Atlantic Monthly has bought a story from me and wants another. Boy! Do I feel swell about it! The Atlantic is not a good magazine but it is an institution in this country and I feel a certain pride in my versatility now that I have cracked it.

I am working on a scenario. I think it is going to go across, since I have shrewdly inserted a Jesuit priest into the yarn and built up a good role for either Jackie Cooper or Frankie Darro.[42] The Catholic church is playing straight into my hands with their absurd censorship. Joe Breen and Cardinal O'Connell will glory in the sight of a Jebbie in the movies.[43]

This is pretty good: When I submitted my scenario to Sam Bischoff,[44] a producer at Warners, I told him my novel was being seriously considered by the Catholic Book Club. Nothing was farther from the truth. The Catholic Book Club would burn my book publicly after reading the first page. Anyhow, Bischoff swallowed the bait and in a frenzy asked to see a copy of the novel. I turned over the script to him, and so help me God, he thinks it's a very edifying Catholic work!

Here's a good one on Erskine Caldwell.[45] He is out here coining money hand over fist at Metro-Goldwyn-Mayer. The producers assigned him to the task of writing an original North Woods story. Caldwell is from the South, as you know. He was stumped. But he went to work and delivered a long script. He had no idea of what a "North Woods" story was about, so, on the last page of his script, the last line, he wrote in parenthesis, "(All of the above action takes place in the North Woods.)"

I met Robert Joyce Tasker. He has gone to pot. He is married to an heiress of the Fletcher's Castoria people. With plenty of dough his brain has gone fat on him. Most of his literary output — in fact all — is done orally at night clubs. He's a handsome fellow, a trifle conceited. His wife is a handsome blonde animal in her middle thirties. Her eyes ooze sex. Tasker is an awful liar. He takes great pride in his stir in the penitentiary. That of course is plausible in this town, but when he says that he and Ernest Booth[46] were members of the same gang of crooks and were sent up for the same charge, it's a patent lie to anyone who knows the facts.

Incidentally, Dr. James McAnally, who sent you (so he told me) Ernest Booth's early manuscripts, is a friend of mine. He lives across the street from my people's ranch in Roseville. According to him — he is a physician at Folsom — Jim Tully's visit there and Tully's report of that visit and of his interview with Booth in the Mercury was so unfair and inaccurate that from the date of its appearance the prison writers to a man have hated Jim Tully's guts.

After that article, Warden Court Smith forbade all interviews and no man with literary ability has been permitted to express himself in publications outside the prison walls. This is obviously narrowness on the part of Court Smith rather than tactlessness on the part of Jim Tully, but I give you the item for whatever it may be worth to you. Doubtlessly you know the facts.

I met a fellow last week named Angelo DeGrando, or some such name. He makes a business of writing celebrated people and then selling their responses. He has hooked you twice, so he laughed, and I feel it is a terribly lousy stunt, particularly in your case, because I know you are such a good fellow and always sincere and anyone so tawdry as to exploit your kindness in that way needs a kick in the teeth. In fact, I told this mug he'd never get another letter from you. I hope you'll recall his name if he tries again. I may be prejudiced, but I would rather those cads pick on somebody else.

It occurs to me that you have tried your hand at every phase of expression except biography. And who is there but you to do a life of George Sterling?[47] He is not as significant perhaps as Bierce or Jack London,[48] but his life was a fascinating one. I have seen some of his letters and they are very lovely. Even a collection of these would be worthwhile. In the Sacramento library I saw a card written by Sterling as an autobiographical note for the California State Literary Society. All it said was, "I am a pupil of Ambrose Bierce." It was dated 1900. I tried to steal that card for you, but failed. Some day I shall try again.

Sincerely,
J. Fante
2316 Clyde Ave.
Los Angeles

44

H. L. MENCKEN

704 CATHEDRAL ST.

BALTIMORE

August 9, 1934

Dear Mr. Fante:

I am delighted to hear that you have broken into the Atlantic Monthly. To be sure, you'll be less at home in it that you were in The American Mercury, but that fact in itself is of some value. I think it is important for a young author to appear in print as often as possible, and in as many different magazines as possible.

The scenario sounds amusing indeed. If the brethren swallow it you'll make a lot of money.

I can't remember DeGrando. Probably he is lying. Certainly I'll be on the watch for him hereafter.

If I ever do a biography it will probably be one of Pontius Pilate — my favorite character in history. He is the only really honest man mentioned in the New Testament. I was on the best of terms with George Sterling, but I really know too little about his life to attempt an account of it.

The weather here in the East has been infernal all summer. In consequence, I have got very little work done.

Sincerely yours,
H. L. Mencken

45

WARNER BROS.

PICTURES, INC.

WEST COAST STUDIOS

BURBANK, CALIFORNIA

August 15th, 1934

Dear Mr. Mencken,

Here I sit, laughing and laughing. I have a secretary and a great big office and a lot of people bow low when I pass, all of them hating my Dago guts.

I not only made these folks swallow that bilge-water but I did it to the tune of $1500, plus $250 a week for an indefinite period. Whoops! I never had so much money in the offing in my life; moreover, if my luck holds good I shall certainly bed Del Rio[49] inside of four weeks. Even as a tiny tot behind the coal shed that woman was my objective, and once I sent her twenty-five cents for her picture. Ah, what an American idyll! I see her daily, eat in the same room with her, ogle her big Rolls-Royce, and having concluded that she's unquestionably the world's worst actress, I am all set to tell her so the very instant I meet her. She's never heard it before in her life, and if it doesn't fetch her then I don't know what will. Yowsah. I'm a monstrous clever fellow.

What a movie! I wrote it for Frankie Darro. They didn't like that. They said Kay Francis.[50] So I wrote it for Kay Francis. Then they said change it to Barbara

Stanwyck.[51] So I'm doing it. The yarn used to be a kid story. Now it's a prison story. Some day it will be King Kong. And all I do is write and laugh and laugh and think of Dolores Del Rio: the sorrows of the river. Sweet river. My river. I'm going swimming in that river. I'm going to navigate that river. I think maybe I shall buy that river. I am like Columbus. I stand at the water's edge and dream. And like my countryman, they shall bring me back in irons. But I love it. I am making history. Also, I am trying to make something else. I am in the movies. *Furor scribendi! Poetica furor!* "And the harpies of the shore shall pluck the eagle of the sea!" And some day, genius that I am, I too shall write, "Roll on, thou dark and deep blue ocean, roll!"[52]

Mr. Mencken, you should come out here and get rich. Your fellow contributor to Liberty, he's here. Mister Erle Stanley Gardner. And then your good friend Walpole, he's here.[53] They've got him locked up somewhere at the M.G.M. lot. He's an advisor. An advisor is one who keeps his mouth shut and collects $2500 a week. A stooge.

What about *The American Language.* Don't lie to me, Mr. Mencken, I *know* you had Jean Harlow in mind when you wrote it! That scene in the beer hall! It's magnificent! Stupendous! Mr. Mencken, we must have your *American Language!* And that jungle scene! Oh my God! It was *made* for Harlow!

I know — and this is a fact — I know a famous screenwriter who wants to do an adaptation of Spengler's *Decline of the West* for Cecil de Mille! Yowsah!

Cordially, and begging your pardon,
J. Fante
c/o Sam Bischoff
Warner's Burbank Studio
Burbank, Calif.

Mr. Mencken, if you are busy or don't feel like it, you don't have to answer my letters.

Mencken's reply and a following letter by Fante prior to Mencken's birthday apparently haven't survived. Mencken turned 54 on September 12, 1934. In a September 13 letter to Knopf, he wrote, "I put in the day rather miserably, for there was a little flare-up of hay fever. However, it was enormously milder than my old bouts, and so I retain my confidence in the vaccines."[54]

46

H. L. MENCKEN
704 CATHEDRAL ST.
BALTIMORE

September 15, 1934

Dear Mr. Fante:

Thanks very much for your reminder of my birthday. I put in the day as usual, at hard work, and scarcely found time for my devotions. I begin to believe that old age is more happy than youth. Certainly I am more comfortable than I used to be.

Sincerely yours,
H. L. Mencken

47

H. L. MENCKEN

704 CATHEDRAL ST.

BALTIMORE

December 26, 1934

Dear Mr. Fante:
    Thanks very much for your reminder of the holiday.
Here's hoping that you are lucky in 1935!

Sincerely yours,
H. L. Mencken

*The year did start with good fortune for Fante who wrote to his
mother on January 24, 1935, that he had started working at Warner
Brothers for $250 a week. He was living in an apartment downtown
for $4 per week.*

48

WARNER BROS.

PICTURES, INC.

WEST COAST STUDIOS

BURBANK, CALIFORNIA

February 15, 1935

Dear Mr. Mencken,

Greetings. Is it true that you're coming out to the Coast? Two people have told me so in the last few weeks and I incline to believe them except that as yet you have not put in an appearance.

I certainly like that little thing "Mr. Kipling" which appeared on the Brains Page of the Los Angeles Examiner. Coming from your pen, it was unusual but not at all surprising.[55]

I finished at Warners a couple of months ago and went East afterwards to Denver, where I felt very lost and sad, Denver being my home town. Shortly after my return I was engaged again by these people on the script of an Italian story dealing with the Mafia. I am collaborating with the very Rev. Joel Sayre, the Man Mountain.[56] Of course you know him. . . . a prince of a guy. He knows more about movies than any man in this town and he can write them standing on his head. I have learned a lot from him.

I do hope very much that you're heading West. For three years I have looked forward to the time when I would have the pleasure of knowing you better.

With very best wishes,
J. Fante

Mencken's wife, Sara, who had been in failing health since their marriage in 1930, died of tuberculosis on May 31, 1935.

49

John Fante

August 14, 1935

Dear Mr. Mencken,

Every time I sit down to write a letter to you I get a feeling that I'm wasting my time and yours. It stops me every time. I can't figure it out, unless it's that, not knowing you personally, I have nothing to say to you. Well, the truth is, I have a lot to say, but I can't seem to get it said.

With the regretful passing of Mrs. Mencken, I felt that it was almost my duty to at least drop you a note telling you that I too felt badly about it, but I somehow couldn't do it because I felt that somehow it was none of my business to intrude my own regrets in a misfortune which in itself was complete.

The same situation exists at this moment. I was sitting here reading a book (it's nearly dawn) and all at once I got the idea again that I ought to write a letter to Mencken. I really do have a lot of things to write about, but for some reason the whole idea of putting them in a letter is absurd. The minute I get going I say to myself, why bother that guy? He's got his own life to live. And so I stop.

When you quit editing the magazine it did me no good, in my opinion. My prejudices were emphatically in your direction and I lost interest in writing. I think this was because I attached more importance to your approval than to the idea of writing, per se. Of course I've written a great deal since then, and when I write a good piece it is bought and published. But there isn't much fun in it anymore. I realize the banality of the situation, or maybe it is adolescence, and so I suppose I'm getting over it.

If I have learned anything in my life it is the knowledge that in life there is no lesson to learn. You simply stick your chin out and take them, one two three. After a while, unless you write a book called *Why Not Try God?* or *Why Die?* you just die, that's all. In either case it's death. But what annoys me is my inability to find anything amusing in great authors like Mary Pickford.[57] If I could get a belly laugh out of her creations, as I think you do, life would certainly be more worthwhile. Instead, reading the Pickford bile, I am convinced that it's simply no use. This conviction has little value unless there is someone to share it. I can't tell my girl about it because she's not interested in my convictions.[58]

In her opinion I ought to keep my mouth shut because, after all, Mary Pickford has written a book and I haven't.

I think what makes life most unbearable is my inability to satisfy my desire for power and attention. Sometimes I hole in for weeks to be alone. After a while I realize why I have done it. Instinctively I have crawled away from the battlefield until my spiritual wounds heal. Some people can cure themselves in public. If I could do it heroically, I too would go in for public exhibitions of rehabilitation. But I never heal nobly. Like a hurt dog, I snarl and yap. This is bad for my reputation, such as it is, and so I want to be alone.

One thing I have learned is that I am not intelligent. Once I was conceited, and this I thought to be intelligence. I don't know how one goes about getting intelligence. You can't do it by reading and writing; if that were true, I could modestly claim a certain brilliance. Every fine book I read tends to reinforce my low opinion of my own mind and makes me envious of the man who wrote it. But it is not the right kind of envy. If it were, I would write by straight imitation; of course I do write from imitation, but only in so far as I can do it without detection, either of myself or the editor.

But writing to you this way gives me a curious feeling of lucidity, a belief in my own power. It is miserably selfish of me to make such an exorbitant request but I can't see any other way out of it. Would you mind receiving letters from me at pretty regular intervals? It would mean an inevitable request that you read copy now and then, particularly since I am writing my second attempt at a novel, which by the way, I'm going to dedicate to you. The first novel was unacceptable. However most of it has been taken by magazines in short story form. This new book is honest to the point of ghastliness.

Sincerely,
J. Fante
Box 1503
Hollywood

50

H. L. MENCKEN

704 CATHEDRAL ST.

BALTIMORE

August 20, 1935

Dear Mr. Fante:

You are going through one of the periods of discontent and impatience that afflict all authors. When you come out of it you'll find that you have learnt something, and that writing will be a shade easier. I see no reason why you shouldn't plant plenty of stuff. Have you ever approached Paul Palmer,[59] my successor on The American Mercury? I think he'd be delighted to hear from you. He is getting out a pretty good magazine, and he tells me that he is very short of manuscript.

It goes without saying that I'll be glad to read your novel when it is ready. Let the manuscript come to me as above and I'll go through it promptly. It is kind of you to think of dedicating it to me.

The works of Pickford, of course, are difficult for such earthworms as you and me. She rises to levels that are really beyond us. I suggest that you go into prayer for ten or twenty days before you tackle her again. Devote yourself to God and you will have a better understanding of His boosters.

I am still grinding away on the rewriting of my old book, The American Language.[60] It was interrupted by my wife's illness and death, but I am now putting in some heavy licks on it, and hope to finish it by the end of the year.

Sincerely yours,
H. L. Mencken

On November 3, 1935, Fante wrote to his mother to say that he was working on a French Foreign Legion story at Republic Studios. He complained of stomach trouble and said he was near collapse. On November 14, he told his mother he had been fired from Republic, and that he was suffering from bleeding gums. In December he apparently sent Mencken a letter about Aimee Semple McPherson (1890–1944), the popular evangelist who founded the Echo Park Evangelist Association in 1921, for which she built Angelus Temple Church of the Foursquare Gospel. She also owned a radio station from which she broadcast her sermons. Fante, at this time, had a landlady who was a fan of McPherson and with whom he debated what he considered the evangelist's rather thin theological precepts. He later incorporated those encounters into his novel, Dreams From Bunker Hill. *McPherson was nationally known, and her radio broadcasts would have caught Mencken's attention. Mencken delighted in reporting on the activities of popular evangelists, whom he more than once labeled mountebanks.*

51

H. L. MENCKEN

704 CATHEDRAL ST.

BALTIMORE

December 24, 1935

Dear Mr. Fante:

My very best thanks. I have read every word of that debate and I leave it more than half convinced that the Bible is true from the first word to the last. Sister Aimee's arguments are simply irresistible. No man with a heart beating seventy times a minute could fail to be fetched by them.

I hope you are lucky in 1936.

Sincerely yours,
H. L. Mencken

In the following letter Fante talks about his novel in progress, which, when finally published posthumously in 1985 was titled The Road to Los Angeles. *Fante is not 23, going on 24; he is 27, going on 28.*

52

Dear Mr. Mencken,

I enclose Part One of the novel I'm dedicating to you. My reason for sending you only a part of it is due to the fact that, although the rest is finished, it is unreadable, and I am impatient to find out what you think of the writing. What follows is even better than the enclosed.

Here's the situation. Three years ago Knopf advanced me 500 dollars on a first novel, which I accepted. Later he sent along another hundred. At the time I sincerely believed I had a novel in my head, but I came to realize soon enough that it would be a lousy one. When I finished it I sent it to him and he was naturally disappointed. To make matters worse, I had been bombarding him with letters telling him what a swell novel I was writing. The build-up went to pieces when he saw what I had written and only made matters worse. That first novel was pretty bad. If Knopf has a bad taste in his mouth as far as I'm concerned, I certainly have no one to blame but myself.

If you like the enclosed, I hope you'll tell Knopf about it. No need to write him a letter, but when you see him I hope you'll tell him you enjoyed what is here. I don't mean this to be a routine soft-soaping testimony because I know you don't do things that way, but if you sincerely think this is good work then it would be appreciated if you said so to Alfred. He will feel better about that six hundred he handed me.

This book is as autobiographical as the reader chooses to take it. The facts though are considerably different than the writing. But psychologically it is as sincerely autobiographical as I could possibly make it. I am not able to say whether or not I have done good work, but if I can hear you say you liked these fifty pages I am confident about the rest, because in contrast it is in my opinion much better.

I am honest about why I wrote this book. I wrote it to get money and recognition as a writer. I wrote it because I lived it and it was comparatively easy to write. If I could have done a book on insect life as easily as this, I would have done so. On the other hand, I would not do a book on insects if I could get more money doing this kind of book. I want a name first. The time for reflection and insect books will come afterward.

I am both a Communist and a Capitalist. And then I am neither. I say to hell with taking sides. That I learned from your writings. I choose to be myself. The extent of that effort is written in the peregrinations of Arturo, my character in the book. He is me, [and you might] say, I am he. I think it a representative picture of my type of young man. I am twenty-three now, soon to be twenty-four. My type of young man is the fellow who fits no notch in these contemporary times except by force. If irony is the fruit of bitterness I suppose I am embittered. But it's too early to say anything yet. Ten years will tell the tale, although there are more reasons for saying I will not be alive in ten years than for saying that I will be alive. History will make me and my type fools, but I know this a long time before the history is written. (I am trying to write a philosophic summary of my book here, in case you're wondering what the hell this is all about.)

I thought of sending you a resume of what happens in the last portions of the book, but I am sure it will not interest you. Briefly though, nothing happens. The boy runs away to Los Angeles and has an unsuccessful love affair and the story concludes on the same note it was begun. He gets nowhere really, but he fulfills a sort of cycle around a given point. Fitting nowhere in the average American scene, the boy becomes a writer, and being no great shakes at this either, he might just as well be back where he started, digging ditches.

I have an extra copy of what is enclosed, so it will be quite alright to destroy this when you finish it. I am calling it "In My Time."

Sincerely,
J. Fante
4671 Hollywood Blvd.
Los Angeles, Calif.

53

H. L. MENCKEN

704 CATHEDRAL ST.

BALTIMORE

March 17, 1936

Dear Mr. Fante:

The only objection to this manuscript that I can unearth is that it is rather long on discussion and short on story. But that is a minor matter. It seems to me to be very interesting stuff, and I see no reason whatever why you shouldn't plant it.

Why do you use such odd manuscript paper? Every

99

time you put a manuscript reader to any inconvenience, however slight, you damage your chances. He much prefers ordinary letter size paper. Moreover, he prefers perfectly clean manuscript, without any corrections. These may seem to be small matters, but they are actually very important.

I am in the last stages of my own book, and it is working me to death.

Sincerely yours,
H. L. Mencken

54

May 30, 1936
Roseville, Cal.

Dear Mr. Mencken,

I would have thanked you long ago for giving me your opinion of my novel, but for three months I have been very sick — stomach — and have done no writing at all.

You didn't say in your letter that you disliked the book, but the implication was there. And I'm sorry. Praise coming from a great man like yourself would have delighted me forever. But for all that, an opinion is an opinion and I thank you for now taking the time to read those 70 pages and make a comment.

I have to disagree with your reaction. Recall that you said the book was long on discussion and short on story. Both Louis Adamic[61] and Carey McWilliams have seen the book, and they incline to disagree; in fact, they think highly of it; which, I suppose, proves nothing.

I understand the revised edition of *The American Language* is now available, and I hear a lot of fine things about it. I am very glad. The book is one of my favorites, I read a bit of it now and then, perhaps once a month I go back to it, not only for what it contains, but also because it is so lovably written. If the revised version is even better than my copy I know there is much in store for me.

Kindest regards,
J. Fante
211 Pleasant St.
Roseville, Calif.

Fante attended the Western Writers Conference in San Francisco on November 13–15, 1936, which he recollects in the following letters. The conference was a politically charged affair. It was chaired by Michael Gold, author of Jews Without Money,[62] *a novel about class struggle in New York City, editor of* The New Masses *and a contributor to* The Daily Worker *up to the end of his life. Fante's close friend Carey McWilliams wrote of the conference in his* Pacific Weekly, *"In retrospect, it will probably be recognized that no more important occurrences broke the darkening circle of post-war reaction than the various national and international congresses of writers, artists and intellectuals called to protest against the social and cultural decay implicit in Fascism." Fante and Mencken both were clearly more skeptical of the outcome of such congresses and this one in particular, which was, given the chairmanship and lineup of speakers, heavily dominated by the far left.*

101

55

Dear Mr. Mencken—

How does everything go with you? I keep wondering what you are doing and hoping that you are alright. I don't write you so many letters anymore because—well—they were pretty asinine letters anyway, and in retrospect I can imagine you considered me a terrible nuisance. It was awfully nice of you not to reveal it. No matter what you wrote me was always deeply appreciated and cherished.

Last night I finished the new *American Language*. It is such a marvelous thing, so full of laughter and wisdom. To have been the author must be a very satisfying pleasure. It is a giant of a book.

I can't say much for my novel. Knopf thought it was horrible stuff and so did Vanguard. But William Soskin[63] is interested. It means months of rewrite though. But writing persists being the thing I like best of all, and so I do not mind. Indeed, I am very grateful for Soskin's interest. Meanwhile I have begun work on another book—I am waiting to hear more from Soskin—and this new book moves along with such ease that I am at a loss to judge it. I have come to hate short-story writing. They are money-getters, and if you can't make the slick sheets you have a hard time. The best way for a writer nowadays to get money is not through short stories but via the movies. Slick sheet short stories are fine if you can do them, but I haven't the patience. When I go broke my agent in Hollywood can usually place me for a few weeks at one of the studios—until they fire me—and I come away with enough to breathe easy. But it's a nerve-racking, jittery existence and in the last analysis not worthwhile. The compromise becomes increasingly difficult. Hollywood is a bad place. It kills writers. They die young and violently down there.

I haven't sucked out on Communism and I can't find much in Fascism. As I near twenty-six, I find myself moving toward marriage and a return to Catholicism. Augustine and Thomas More knew the answers a long time ago. Aristotle would have spat in Mussolini's face and sneered at Marx. The early fathers would have laughed themselves sick over the New Deal and Coughlin.[64] The demagogues and phonies get in my hair. I am losing my patience. If I get ahold of enough money, I may leave the country. Give me a few books, some wine, a girl, and a bit of good music. The sheep will be stamped out and die anyhow. All I want is that they leave me alone. Nowadays, to hear people talk, you wouldn't know that great men have lived and written fine books and wonderful music. World history seems to have begun with Kerensky and ended with Hitler.[65] Fuck it.

I don't know what happened to Joel Sayre. He got out of Hollywood with a big pile of money and went to Mexico. He and William Faulkner did a movie called The Road to Glory for Zanuck. It began with great possibilities, but the end was a mixture of O. Henry and Bill Faulkner; it was twisty and I think goofy. But it made money, so what the answer.[66]

Beginning Thursday the writers of the West are having a convention in San Francisco. Everybody will be there, and my hope is that it takes on the finale of an American Legion shindig. But it looks bad from the program. Mike Gold is delivering a "Message to the West"; Upton Sinclair will instruct us on "How to Fight Fascism," and phonies like John Bright, Robert Tasker, Nat West (scenario writers) will give us the low-down on what great literature is about. Papers will be read on "Fascist Trends,"

"Economics of the Writing Profession" and "Creative Problems and Criticism." It is my first convention, and I hope to learn a lot.[67]

Sincere good wishes,
J. Fante
211 Pleasant St.
Roseville, Calif.

56

H. L. MENCKEN

1524 HOLLINS ST.

BALTIMORE

November 18, 1936

Dear Mr. Fante:

I certainly agree with your feeling about the Communists and Fascists, though I fear I can't follow you into the arms of Holy Church. All persons who propose to improve the human race seem to me to be equally fraudulent. It makes progress undoubtedly, but that progress is due a great deal less to exhortation than to simple evolution. My belief is that it will go so far that in another ten or twenty thousand years at least 10% of the human beings living on earth will be as intelligent as the average horse and as decent as the average dog. I may be optimistic, but such is my belief.

I am glad that you have fallen into the hands of Soskin. He is a very intelligent man, and I believe that he'll do well with his new publishing house. In his days as a reviewer he always steered clear of the crazes that periodically afflicted his colleagues.

That writers' conference at San Francisco must have been completely dreadful. All of the great geniuses you mention are notorious quacks. I wish I could have got into the hall anonymously and heard the sermons.

Sincerely yours,
H. L. Mencken

57

Nov. 24, 1936

Dear Mr. Mencken —

Indeed you would have enjoyed the Writer's Conference in San Francisco had you been there anonymously. I personally was disappointed with the thing as a whole, but in part the affair had some real laughs. My experience with writers is invariably disillusioning. The more I meet them the less I think of the profession. There is always the man's work — and then the man. That is excusable in hacks and to be expected, but it seems to me the messiah on paper should not step out of his role in real life. Mike Gold for example turns out to be a platitude carrying a cross. He's so god-awful paternalistic, and yet so unmistakably adolescent. Ella Winter, the poetess, is a bustling old dame in a gypsy costume who bows her head reverently whenever you mention the word Steffens. The Great Muckraker (God rest his bones) was certainly taken; for the life of me I can't figure it out. Having read his autobiography and then met his mate, I can't help but wonder what the hell it's all about.[68]

Charles Erskine Scott Wood is an old man who has grown a Whitman beard and does a competent job of playing the role of Moses with a sense of humor.[69]

Everyone in the hall was compelled to stand up and cheer in the "Star Spangled Banner" manner when the old boy creaked out the back way. It was most embarrassing—particularly to me, for I know the old codger is as phony as a press-agent. I did, however, enjoy his amazing complacency in all that racket. Now he will die convinced of his immortality. That, too, shall be sweet, triumphant and phony.

Father Gold was chairman of the proceedings. I attended only one lecture, observed that the women were horrible and hard-boiled, and left. But that one lecture was pretty swell fun. The question—among others—was, "What are we to do about our unfortunate comrades in Hollywood, the scenario writers?"

Dorothy Parker, who is evidently "in sympathy" with the proletariat, breezed into the hall wearing a Hollywood fur coat that must have cost easily two grand, and promptly the poor red women sighed adoringly.[70] It might have been Garbo herself. Parker is supposed to be a regular heller at cutting people down with her Shenee sarcasm, and everybody waited breathlessly for the big moment. But no. Parker was Garbo tonight. When they gave her the soapbox she managed a sobby delivery and asked the comrades to sympathize with the poor scenarists; she admitted they made big money, but there was nothing that could be done about it. She led the wild-eyed Reds to believe that

Marxism was not dead in Hollywood, that with a pinch here and a pinch there the scenarists were cautiously sowing the seeds of rebellion. The movement was underground, but that was necessary. All of which is twaddle. It was the Capitalistic coat that put her across. Even Father Gold betrayed a trifle too much interest in it, but he caught himself just in time and turned on the paternalism. He's very good at it!

Poor Carey McWilliams was the sucker. I stayed with him in San Francisco and got a pretty good idea of what the Reds will do to an agreeable and curious man. Carey is more pink than Red and after three days of slavery for those longhairs they made him editor of a dozen different pamphlets, programs, brochures, magazines and papers. Not only that, but chairman of fifty different committees. He has enough work — without pay — to keep him busier for a full year than Lenin during the Ten Days. When he left to catch the Los Angeles train he was sweating beneath the weight of a portfolio that might have been a bale of hay. I think they made a Fascist out of him.

As far as I am concerned the conference was a success because I got a chance to talk with this fellow Harry Bridges.[71] I thought he was hawk-faced, sharp, intelligent and terrifically conceited. McWilliams threw a lot of questions at him which he answered with insolent finality. Apparently the reason the Federals haven't muscled into the present waterfront strike is the President's promise not to interfere provided they backed him in the last election, which they did to a man.

Bridges is my idea of a sourpuss who would make a first-class dictator. McWilliams tripped him up a couple of times and he promptly put on a Hitler scowl and turned on the sneer. He's a good man for the stevedores: one of

those rare people who won't sell out under any cir-
cumstances. He must be forty-two, a tall bundle of nerves,
humorless as a stomach pump.

With best personal wishes,
J. Fante
211 Pleasant St.
Roseville, Calif.

58

H. L. MENCKEN

1524 HOLLINS ST.

BALTIMORE

December 5, 1936

Dear Mr. Fante:
Your description of the writers' conference is swell indeed. Why don't you make an article of it and send it to
Bernard DeVoto, editor of the Saturday Review of
Literature, or to Paul Palmer, editor of the American Mercury? I believe that either or both of them would be immensely interested. The Communist papers, of course,
have treated the conference with the utmost gravity. Obviously, any gathering operated by Mike Gold must have
been full of unconscious comedy.

I have just got home after a week in New York. I always leave the town with immense relief. It is gradually becoming completely uninhabitable.

Sincerely yours,
H. L. Mencken

59

Jan. 11, 1937

Dear Mr. Mencken —

What has become of your manuscript *Advice to Young Men*?[72] If you don't get it out soon it will be valueless in this case of one young man at least. From a selling point, such a book ought to be very successful these days.

I have resigned myself to Roseville and I don't think I'll ever return to Hollywood unless they prove they want me with a good offer. Hollywood is not so difficult for the writer as it is for his nervous system. My guess is that the mortality rate among the scribblers is both high and premature. In a town of thousands of writers, I doubt that you could find more than a dozen over fifty-five who are still producing. I may be prejudiced, but I don't think so. When I speak of the Hollywood writer I mean, of course, the scenarist.

It hits the stomach first: nervous indigestion. Every writer I know has been hit more or less by it. Nor am I an exception. I thought it was my heart. No less than seven doctors told me that for the last seven months I haven't been dying. The mysterious connection between the kidneys and the ability to write is one of the ironic tragedies of this business. I never believed it until it hit me. The only cure on earth is starvation. If you're ever attacked, lay off food as much as possible and you'll live. This is my own personal remedy, and it succeeded where diets and pills failed.

I was very low and broke Dec. 24, in the morning. It looked like a terrible Christmas. Then, in the afternoon mail I got the biggest kick of my career. Three acceptances! The Atlantic Monthly, The American Mercury, and Scribners! All in the same mail—that's really hitting the ball. Those acceptances, plus the starvation diet, lifted me from the grave and after seven months I am now a well man.

I was loop-eyed from Scotch both Xmas and New Year, but I didn't have so much as a headache afterwards.

In your *Advice for Young Men* I hope you warn them against the writing business. It's too tough. I'm definitely in now that my scope has broadened to the conception of novels and I reckon I'll stick it out to the bitter end, but if I ever have a son he will not write for a living. Thank God the novel is washed up as an art form. For, if my son *should* write, it won't be in the composition of crap. Maybe the historian and critic has a better time of it. Which reminds me that, alas, last week I finished one novel and immediately began the revision of another. It has taken me four years to realize that what I want most from art is money. I'll get it too, and plenty of it, if my kidneys and liver hold out.

Regards,
J. Fante
Box 498
Roseville,
Calif.

60

H. L. MENCKEN

1524 HOLLINS ST.

BALTIMORE

January 22, 1937

Dear Mr. Fante:

I surely hope that living at Rosewood[73] will produce a rapid cure. My belief is that if I had to stay in Hollywood I'd be dead in six months.

A week or two before Christmas I was floored by a throat infection, and spent the holidays in hospital. It turned out to be anything but bad — in fact, my Christmas in bed was the best I had spent since childhood. All of the usual hooey was missing, and I put in a quiet and peaceful day.

Sincerely yours,
H. L. Mencken

The letters below indicate that Fante sent Mencken clippings per-taining to the publication of a reportedly newly discovered O. Henry (William Sydney Porter: 1862–1910) story in the January, 1937, edition of Redbook *magazine. Over the months the magazine printed four more of the stories.* Literary Digest *on April 10, 1937, ex-plained that the stories were discovered by a graduate student whose grandfather worked at the* Houston Post. *While visiting the paper, the student found the stories, which ran without bylines, but were in the O. Henry style and published while he worked at the paper. Their authenticity was never proven, and the stories weren't generally considered up to the author's capabilities. In* The Complete Works of O. Henry *editor Harry Hansen omitted the stories, claiming, "they are of indifferent quality and not positively identified as his."*[74]

61

H. L. MENCKEN

1524 HOLLINS ST.

BALTIMORE

February 23, 1937

Dear Mr. Fante:

Thanks very much for the clippings. It seems almost incredible that O. Henry should have left any unpublished short stories. He was always no more than half a leap ahead of his editors. Many a time a magazine had to be held up for two or three days to wait for his manuscript. I simply can't imagine how he should have accumulated any un-published stuff.

Sincerely yours,
H. L. Mencken

62

JOHN FANTE

3/24/37

Dear Mr. Mencken —

I must have sucked out completely on the Red Book O. Henry hoax, but it appeared authentic to me, with one exception: the "discoverer" of the "heretofore unpublished stories" was not mentioned in name, although her picture was attached. She was such a gorgeous bessie that I momentarily suspected the whole set-up.

Doc McAnally, attached to the hospital force at Folsom, told me yesterday of the ironical misfortunes beset-ting Ernest Booth. According to the doc, Booth is watched incessantly, for he is full of amazing tricks, one of which has been his repeated efforts to attract sympathy and leni-ency by contracting, or at least showing symptoms of, tuberculosis. I don't know what happens when a convict does contract the disease, but I guess the parole board gives victims special consideration while the doctors confine patients to the prison hospital, where life is more pleasant than in the cell blocks, where the jute mill routine is emphasized. Anyhow, there must be plenty of TB in Folsom. It seems Booth has been trying to convince the medicos that he, too, belongs in the TB ward. According to the doc, he went so far as to bring to the hospital the sputum of a bona fide sufferer, claiming it to be his own, but the deception was discovered.

Now, ironically enough, Booth *has* got tuberculosis! Worse, he has contracted a particularly pernicious and painful brand of it. The doc is not very sympathetic. He feels that Booth's stunts are on the whole rather infantile, that *per se,* his cleverness is of a somewhat low order; however, the matter is completely out of his hands. He merely works there. He feels that, now that Booth is a sick man, the best place for him is Folsom. I take it from him that whenever a convict is shown special consideration for parole by virtue of his tubercular condition, the worst place for the sick man is beyond prison walls and freedom. He doesn't take care of himself as he is forced to do in the penitentiary, and his finish is altogether too premature.

I never thought much of Booth as a writer; indeed, I always felt that his stuff was rewritten. But aside from my opinion of his talent, bank robber and scribbler, he seems to have had a lousy deal from the first hand; his life is a horror story in the extreme. And yet I suppose the answer to it all is that he asked for it.

Best regards,
J. Fante
Box 498
Roseville
Calif.

63

John Fante, Esq.,
Box 498
Roseville, Calif.

Dear Mr. Fante:

When Booth concocted his crazy scheme to get out of prison by changing the record in his case I lost interest in him. His wife writes to me occasionally, but her plans for helping him seem to be very vague and I must add not very promising. Jim Tully, who went to see him some years ago, came away with the feeling that he ought to be kept in jail. He is probably an incurably dangerous man. It is too bad that he has tuberculosis, but he'll certainly get just as good treatment in Folsom as he'd be likely to get outside. I never hear from him directly, but only through his wife.

The O. Henry business remains mysterious. I find it impossible to believe that O. Henry actually left unpublished manuscripts. He was always behind hand with his deliveries. Moreover, he was always so hard up that it is inconceivable that he should have failed to try to sell anything that he had written.

Sincerely yours,
H. L. Mencken

In the next letter Fante announces his marriage to Joyce Smart on July 31, 1937. Smart was a poet and a graduate of Stanford University, and a native of Roseville, California, where Fante often visited his family. The book Fante refers to is Wait Until Spring, Bandini, *published by Stackpole & Sons in 1938.* Pater Doloroso *and* The Road to Los Angeles *had been rejected by Knopf and* The Road to Los Angeles *was rejected by a half-dozen other publishers, most likely because of the explicit language and subject matter and the unconscionable character of the protagonist, the young Arturo Bandini. The manuscript of* The Road to Los Angeles *was submitted by Joyce Fante to Black Sparrow Press after her husband's death, and published by the firm in 1985.*

64

JOHN FANTE

3/20/38

Dear Mr. Mencken,

I thoroughly enjoyed your editorial in the Sun for March 4th. It should be published in pamphlet form and sent to all points in the nation.[75]

I was recently married to Joyce Smart, a Stanford girl who writes wonderful poetry and is also very remarkable in a kitchen apron. We live here in Los Angeles, where

I am writing a novel which William Soskin will print in the fall. I trust you are in good health and ever the Mencken fighting man.

With best of luck,
J. Fante
206 North New Hampshire, #106
Los Angeles, California

65

March 24 [1938]

Dear Mr. Mencken,

Over a period of years I've made many sporadic readings of Nietzsche, especially *Thus Spake Zarathustra*, but recently I decided to read all of the Nietzsche output. I find, however, that it is no easy job to sit down and try to enjoy a book like *Beyond Good and Evil*. Obviously, to understand that work requires more than a casual interest in the philosopher. He makes this quite clear himself in an early passage of *Beyond Good and Evil* when he writes that, if the book is too tough for the reader, it is certainly not his (Nietzsche's) fault. Then he goes on to say that to really understand *Beyond Good and Evil*, the reader must have thoroughly digested and understood *Thus Spake Zarathustra*.

In my opinion he is wrong; for, indeed, there are many passages of *Thus Spake Zarathustra* which are equally as obscure as anything the man ever wrote: for example, what the hell is the philosopher of the "Superman" talking about in this passage from *Zarathustra*, Part 4, LXIII? "The peasant is at present the best; and the peasant type should be master! But it is the kingdom of the populace—I no longer allow anything to be imposed upon me. The populace, however—that meaneth hodgepodge."

For that matter all of LXIII, "Talk With Kings," is hodgepodge. And yet it contains here and there more Marxian dynamite than the Reds ever dreamed about. That is quite beside the point. What I should like to get from you is a reading prospectus of the works of Nietzsche, based upon your wide familiarity with everything he has written. I think Wright once suggested a reading approach, but as I remember it didn't seem to satisfy me.[76]

If you can find the time to do this for me—fine and dandy. If not, but sure that I can readily understand that you're a busy man. Thanks.

Sincerely yours,
J. Fante
206 North New Hampshire, #106
Los Angeles

66

The Evening Sun

Sun Square

Baltimore, Md.

Editorial Department

March 29, 1938

Dear Mr. Fante:

I offer you my most sincere congratulations, but have only condolences for your poor wife. She will discover soon enough that living with a literary gent is a dreadful experience. I only hope that she is never tempted to load your victuals with roach powder.

I am delighted to hear about the novel. If you stick to it you'll make a good one.

Sincerely yours,
H. L. Mencken

67

The Evening Sun

Sun Square

Baltimore, Md.

Editorial Department

March 30, 1938

Dear Mr. Fante:

I agree with you thoroughly that there is a great deal of bosh in Nietzsche. Worse, the bosh occurs in the midst of his very best stuff. Thus, there is no way to read him without swallowing the whole together. Fortunately, the total range of his books is not great and you can plow through them in a couple of months. There is enough really first-rate stuff in them to justify the labor.

I wrote a book on him in my younger days, but it is now hopelessly out of date.[77]

Sincerely yours,
H. L. Mencken

68

JOHN FANTE

Dear Mr. Mencken:

Bill Soskin is putting out my first novel in October. You might recall that this is the third try I have had at book-writing, two other attempts having failed. Such a record measures perfectly with your comment that a writer should discard his first two books and get into print with his third.

I had such bad luck with my first two books — both of which I dedicated to you — that I took no chances with the third, for I suspected not only bad writing in each case, but also the evil eye. This time I dedicated the work to my parents, a more fitting gesture — although such things really don't matter.

I am very excited about my first book. I am jittery as I await the proofs. It is a wonderful feeling. The book has a fine title: *Wait Until Spring, Bandini.* Bill Soskin likes it very much. He also has my second attempt at a novel, which I plan to rework and publish next spring. He likes a great deal of it, but not all.

Marriage is alright, Mr. Mencken. It keeps a man satisfied and full of big ideas. I hope my book makes a lot of money so I can travel a bit and develop my ideas. I hope you read it — I'll send you a copy — and though I have not the temerity to suggest that you review it, I hope you will get behind it and tell other people to buy it. If you don't like the book, then by all means warn people against it. I have great faith in it.

Sincerely,
J. Fante
206 North New Hampshire
L.A.

69

H. L. MENCKEN

1524 HOLLINS ST.

BALTIMORE

August 29, 1938

Dear Mr. Fante:

I needn't tell you that I'll read that novel with the greatest interest. If Soskin passes it, then it will be worth printing. My chaplain is instructed to pray for it diligently.

Unfortunately, I won't be able to review it, for I forswore book reviews five years ago and have stuck to my oath. I spent twenty-five years doing them, and that was enough.

Good luck!

Sincerely yours,
H. L. Mencken

In 1940 Fante collaborated with Ross Wills on the film East of the River. *Fante's second novel,* Ask the Dust, *was published by Stackpole in 1939. Shortly after releasing the novel, Stackpole was sued by Adolf Hitler and the German government for infringement of copyright for unauthorized publication of* Mein Kampf. *The Germans won the suit, resulting in financial ruin for the publisher and, Fante believed, lack of adequate promotion of* Ask the Dust. *Black Sparrow reissued the book in 1980.*

Happy Days was the first volume of Mencken's three-part memoirs, which finally included Newspaper Days *and* Heathen Days. *There is no record of the Ross B. Wills writing mentioned in the letter below. This letter, ten years into Mencken and Fante's correspondence, indicates a maturing of the young writer who once wrote bombastic entreaties to his editor.*

70

July 8, 1940

Dear Mr. Mencken,

I am enclosing a swell job of writing and reasoning by a friend of mine, Ross B. Wills, who, by the way, is a great Mencken rooter. I should like you to read his piece.

I don't see much of you in print anymore. Maybe it's because I don't read the right books and magazines. I did read *Happy Days,* which both myself and my wife enjoyed tremendously. We particularly enjoyed the unpretentiousness with which you handled your early life. There was something wonderfully healthy and charming about it all, and I couldn't help thinking of Mark Twain as I read it. We both hope future additions to your autobiography will be as delightful as *Happy Days*.

Myself, I have written two novels. They both made a little money and got a lot of attention. Looking back, I detest the first novel and think the second better than people imagine. But I can't shove my stuff down the public's throat, much as I should like to do so. My third book, entitled *Dago Red,* will be on the Viking fall list. It is composed of short stories, most of which you printed in the Mercury.

I should like very much to hear from you. I miss you editorially and as an iconoclast. I think everybody misses you. I wish to God you'd get back into the magazine business. You're the only guy who really knows the game.

Best wishes, always,
J. Fante
211 Pleasant St.
Roseville, Calif.

71

H. L. MENCKEN

1524 HOLLINS ST.

BALTIMORE

August 1, 1940

Dear Mr. Fante:

I find your pleasant note on my return from New York. Needless to say, I agree with you that the Wills article is excellent stuff. There is no more chance of a revolution in Europe at this minute than there is of a revolution in Hell.

I hope you don't waste any time on the current magazines. I have to see some of them for trade reasons, and the job of going through them is usually very fatiguing. What they all appear to lack is simply ideas.

I had a lot of fun writing *Happy Days* — in fact, so much that I am thinking of doing another volume. That second volume will not deal with my childhood, but with my early newspaper days. Instead of filling it with highfalutin blather about what Roosevelt the elder told me, and how I was entrusted with confidential information by Kaiser Wilhelm and the Pope, I'll devote it wholly to the roaring good time that a young reporter had in those days. It was perhaps the most pleasant period in the whole history of the United States. There were very few telephones and no automobiles at all, and nearly all labor leaders were safe in jail.

I am doing nothing in the way of current journalism save a weekly article for my old paper, the Baltimore Sun. I enclose a few specimens.

Sincerely yours,
H. L. Mencken

72

John Fante
August 6, 1940

Dear Mr. Mencken,

I loved your articles from the Sun. I am only sorry they don't have a wider audience. The prophets and experts of these nasty times are such a lugubrious, pro-British lot that stuff like yours is unique. I wish you could unlimber on some of these sages. I refer to that asshole Kaltenborn and other impresarios of radio propaganda. Frankly, he makes my balls ache. Fifteen minutes a day that fussy old blatherskite has at the American people and his following is simply too depressing to think about. The enormity of the damage he does can scarcely be estimated. The sanctity with which dimwits and mouth-breathers swallow his blah is but another example of the hopeless gullibility of the American people. How does an old fool like Kaltenborn and others like him qualify for the job? Who is the super-expert who selects the experts? If the Americans will eat his *pasta e fagioli,* they'll swallow anything. Elmer Davis,

Raymond Gram Swing, Wythe Williams, John Gunther, Paul Sullivan, John B. Hughes: If they are not salaried by the British Foreign Office, they should smarten up and ask for a cut.[78] Hero-dough is cheap as hell these days. Even Hollywood actors are capitalizing on the war and grabbing all the publicity that phony volunteering will bring.

Your stuff on Franklin, Rex, is a small voice these days. In this connection, I am offering you an idea, one that you could utilize in the fashion of Mark Twain. It should be called "The War Diary of a President." It would run something like this:

September 5. Have written a letter to Hitler, advising him on all matters concerning the German state.

September 7. Have written a letter to Mussolini. Denounced him vigorously for associating with Hitler.

September 9. Have cabled my love to the King and Queen of England. Told them to be patient.

September 11. Hitler's activities very disturbing. Have written him a very strong letter, full of sound advice.

September 12. Decided today to write another letter to Mussolini.

September 15. Mussolini has refused to betray Hitler, as I suggested. I wrote him a powerful letter.

September 16. My new letter to Mussolini has created a sensation both here and in the motherland. This is fun.

September 17. Sleepless night. To amuse myself I wrote a number of savage letters to Mussolini, Hitler, and the King of Japan. Sent a note of affection to the King and Queen of England.

September 20. Thinking of a super-letter to Hitler. If I keep this up, we'll be at war yet.

September 21. Still working on my master-letter to Hitler. Have coined some dandy phrases like, "The hand that held the daggah has thrust it in the back of its neighbah."

September 24. Finished my letter to Hitler.

September 26. Called out the National Guard, in preparation for Hitler's reply to my letter.

September 27. Mailed letter to Hitler.

September 30. Hurray! Hitler has declared war! Received congratulations from the King and Queen.

October 1. It seems we haven't got an army.

October 2. Spent 7 billions ordering an army. This is lots of fun.

October 5. Spent another 4 billion for the army. Ordered army delivered in three weeks, and spare no cost. . . .

    etc., etc.

This is sketchy, but with you doing it, a lot of amusing skulduggery from the record would be included. I hope you can use it sometime.[79]

Sincerely yours,
J. Fante
211 Pleasant St.
Roseville, Calif.

73

H. L. MENCKEN

1524 HOLLINS ST.

BALTIMORE

August 13, 1940

Dear Mr. Fante:

That scheme for a diary is swell. Why don't you execute it yourself? I have so many irons in the fire that I hesitate to take on anything new.

I know absolutely nothing about the radio quacks you mention, for I never listen to the radio. I'd as lief go to a Christian Endeavor meeting. The result of the war will not be determined by the moanings of American crooners, but by the skill and pertinacity of German, Italian and Jap soldiers. Whether or not Roosevelt will get into the thing remains to be seen. He will certainly make the effort. During the last two weeks of the campaign he'll be on the air every night trying to convince the boobs that Hitler is about to bomb Omaha, and that all the Italians in New York are preparing to rise up and massacre the Jews.

Sincerely yours,
H. L. Mencken

74

October 25, 1940

Dear Mr. Mencken,

One of these gloomy days, one Henry Allen Moe, of the Guggenheim Foundation, will take pen in hand to write you a letter requesting your opinion of John Fante as a writer. This is all due to the fact that I am planning to write a novel about the Filipino in California.[80] Spare me your kidney punches, if you will, and tell the gentleman all the good things you can about me. I will appreciate this very much, and the next time I make a novena you can be sure that our blessed Lord will get an earful of some wonderful remarks about H. L. Mencken.

Sincerely yours,
J. Fante
211 Pleasant St.
Roseville, Calif.

75

John Fante

November 9, 1940

Dear H L M:

I am very grateful to you for your willingness to say a word on my behalf to the Guggenheim Foundation. The Filipino story in California is so fantastic, so tragically amusing, that it will take all the restraint I can muster to keep my enthusiasm down to a sane perspective.

For example, one Filipino I know is very bitter about his first experience in America; indeed, it happened the moment he disembarked at San Francisco, where he was met by a high-powered book salesman who immediately sold him an 18-volume work entitled "How to be a Success in America." This relentless scoundrel plagued the poor frightened Filipino into buying it, after chasing him for two miles up Market Street. The Filipino had no money and no job, and therefore could not consummate the deal. This didn't disturb the salesman. He promised the Filipino a job at 12 dollars a week, provided the Pinoy would buy the books. So the deal was made, and the salesman got a job for the Filipino at a disreputable hotel.

The job completely mystified the Filipino. He was supposed to go downstairs to the hotel register each morning, learn what rooms had been rented, and go to those rooms and make the beds. But the beds were always made! The rooms were always rented, the bed was but slightly ruffled each time, and the Filipino scratched his head and wondered at the strange customs of America. And every night the poor guy locked himself in his room and pored over his 18-volume set of books and felt that he was really getting somewhere in this country. That mysterious, distant laughter coming from the corridors often puzzled him — the laughter of women, and sometimes the sound of running and swearing. When he found out that the place was a whorehouse, he quit in outraged horror and fled to Alaska to work in the fish canneries. The fellow told me this with tears in his eyes, but I couldn't help laughing, about that goddamn salesman. I should like to have known the slicker.

How you could have traveled the length and breadth of the land with Crusader Willkie and not advised him on the patent blunders of his campaign is something I don't understand. Myself, I voted for F.D.R. Willkie was too serious for me, too messianic. A veteran with your scars should have whispered in his ear. You might even have written his speeches, which were sloppy, repetitious, monotonous, humorless, terror-mongering, banal. The man lacked humor. He lacked the clown aspect. The city slicker charm of FDR. The Republican campaign should have been a Roman holiday, with laughter and music and plenty of spoofing, plenty of good spirits. Surely you were aware of this. I heard Willkie every time he broadcast, and the more he talked the less he impressed me. I was simply astonished. I had heard that he was decently read, but no man is decently read, and certainly not qualified for a political battle in this country without laughter.

Old Irvin Cobb, even he was deadly serious about the whole thing.[81] He threw in a few Cobb jokes, which, of course, stink; but in the main there was murder in his heart and the humor was not there. Myself, I never ran for any kind of office in my life, but I should like to have been in Willkie's boots, merely to prove my point. I would have had you in there, with Frank Sullivan and maybe Thurber,[82] and I would have slaughtered the New Deal with laughter. I quote you when I say that ridicule and laughter are invincible.

Best regards,
J. F.
211 Pleasant St.
Roseville, Calif.

76

H. L. MENCKEN

1524 HOLLINS ST.

BALTIMORE

November 15, 1940

Dear Mr. Fante:

I agree with you thoroughly, but it was no part of my business to advise Willkie—in fact, I diligently avoided offering him any suggestions. He is a charming fellow, but his political sagacity is not of much horsepower. If he learns the game he may turn out to be a formidable opponent of Roosevelt in 1944, but I am in some doubt that he will learn. In all probability, some new and shrewder fellow will pop up in his place, just as he popped up in Alf Landon's.

I have not yet heard from Moe. As soon as he sends in his questionnaire I'll fill it out in high astounding terms. The best of luck to you![83]

Sincerely yours,
H. L. Mencken

There was no correspondence between Mencken and Fante through the remainder of the 1940s. During the decade Fante wrote stories for The Saturday Evening Post, Woman's Home Companion, Good Housekeeping *and screenplays including* Youth Runs Wild *and* My Man and I. *In 1941 he collaborated with Norman Foster on a screenplay,* My Friend Bonito, *for an Orson Welles project that never materialized. Three sons and a daughter were born to Fante and his wife, Joyce. Joyce Fante said her husband was unhappy with film work and dissatisfied with all of his script projects, except* Full of Life, *mentioned below.*

The decade was an active one for Mencken, though his presence as a public figure declined as he retreated to Hollins Street to write his memoirs and complete other major writing projects. He published A New Dictionary of Quotations *in 1942 and his third autobiographical work,* Heathen Days, *in 1943. A Christmas Story was released in 1946. His collection of favorite early writings was published as* A Mencken Chrestomathy *in 1949. He covered his last Presidential conventions in 1948, sending articles to the Baltimore Sun from June to November of that year, which were later synthesized into* Mencken's Last Campaign. *Mencken was immobilized by a stroke on November 23, 1948, just after covering his last campaign. His condition gradually worsened to the point that he could finally no longer read, write or speak.*

The letter below was apparently prompted by something Fante read about Mencken's condition. Mencken would have probably been amused by Fante's claim to have returned to the church, a claim Joyce Fante believes to be untrue.

77

June 18, 1951

Dear Mr. Mencken,

All I know of you these days is what I read in the papers, but no news is indeed good news and I hope this finds you over the hump.

Your trouble of course rises from a dissolute life and those enemies of yours still alive will hang grimly to salute that day when the Devil shall claim you. Myself, when I read of your rough going, came up with a few prayers which might have helped a bit for all I know. I have returned to the Church, which I find as cantankerous as ever, as unyielding and irritating as in the days of my adolescence. But I must face it: the Church is my home. I love it.

It is surely twelve years since I wrote you a letter. In that time I have acquired a wife and four children, and lost my father, who died six months ago at 72. I suppose the most wonderful event of my life was the birth of my first boy. I am sure the greatest pain came with the loss of my father.

My new novel, and the first in 10 years, and the best by far, is being published by Little, Brown in the fall. The dedication will read:

For H. L. Mencken, in undiminished admiration.

Regards always,
John Fante
625 South Van Ness Ave.
Los Angeles 5, Calif.

I have never been east of North Platte, Nebraska. But this year I might venture into the Eastern hinterland, even to Baltimore. I shall bring not one but two women for you, and we will have a ball.

78

March 21, 1952

Dear Mr. Mencken,

Today I am sending you a copy of my book *Full of Life,* which I dedicated, with much satisfaction, to you. God knows whether or not you'll like the book, but I can assure you it was written with much zest and pleasure.

I think you will be interested in the spiritual and financial history of this ribald little tome. I wrote it as a short story last spring, but my agent got Woman's Home Companion interested in publishing an expanded version, for which they gave me a couple of thousand in advance.

The magazine rejected my final version, however, and Little, Brown agreed to publish it. While still in manuscript form I peddled it to Stanley Kramer[84] of the films for forty thousand bucks. Last month Reader's Digest decided to run about 7000 words of the novel in their May issue, for which they presented me with an additional 7000 dollars. All of these monies, plus what I got from Little, Brown in the form of an advance gives me a total of 50 grand for a book that has yet to be put on the market. Needless to say, the case history of this little book adds up to absolutely nothing, unless it be that success in this business is a matter of incredible luck.

I must admit that I made one rather embarrassing compromise along the way. The book is fiction, pure and simple. Little, Brown felt that as fiction it would not sell. They wondered if I would object to using my own name for the hero. I went along. Now, by virtue of this absurd change in names, the book is no longer fiction but fact.

How does it go with you? I trust this letter finds you well over the hump, and that the great courage so lavish in your writings is also there to beat back what must be a fearful siege. God be with you on the road back to victorious health.

Sincerely yours,
John Fante
28981 W. Cliffside Dr.
Route 2
Malibu, California

79

H. L. MENCKEN

1524 HOLLINS ST.

BALTIMORE-23

March 29, 1952

Dear Mr. Fante:

Mr. Mencken, unfortunately, is still ill and it is quite impossible for him to write to you. But he is certainly delighted to hear that Little Brown has published your book and that you have sold the manuscript to Stanley Kramer for such a handsome price. He surely hopes that the book has a big sale. Mr. Mencken can't read the book at this time, but if he sufficiently recovers to do so sometime later in the year he will certainly go through it with the greatest pleasure. Meanwhile, he sends his hearty congratulations.

Sincerely yours,
Rosalind Lohrfinck
Secretary to Mr. Mencken

80

April 2nd, 1952

Dear Miss Lorhfinck,

Mr. Mencken's condition is very disturbing. As an old admirer with a relationship dating back to 1930 I find it most painful that this great man is apparently unable to read, and obviously unable to write.

Needless to say, I don't care whether or not he can get to the book which I dedicated to him, for it is of no great importance in itself.

Would it be possible to have a note from you, telling me a little more about Mr. Mencken's illness, and of his chances for improvement? I know it must sound absurd, but is there anything, big or small, that might bring him a bit of pleasure?

I am planning a trip to New York soon — the week of April 21st. I had hoped to drop down to Baltimore, but I must assume from your letter that Mr. Mencken's illness makes visitors impossible.

Mr. Mencken is very fond of music. Is he able to listen to recordings? Would it be wise to send him something like that?

Sincerely yours,
John Fante
28981 W. Cliffside Dr.
Route 2
Malibu, California

139

81

H. L. MENCKEN

1524 HOLLINS ST.

BALTIMORE-23

April 7, 1952

Dear Mr. Fante:

Thanks very much for your letter. I am sorry indeed, but Mr. Mencken's condition is such that it would be unwise for you to drop down to Baltimore to see him at this time. Mr. Mencken had a cerebral hemorrhage three years ago and a year later he suffered a severe heart attack. Miraculously, he survived but his condition is very far from good and he can't read anything at all. Please don't send him anything at all. It is kind of you to think of him, but presents embarrass and upset him.

I have just finished reading *Full of Life,* and greatly enjoyed it. The characterization of your father is really superb and I offer my sincere congratulations on a fine piece of work. Mr. Mencken was naturally delighted to have the dedicated copy of the book.

Sincerely yours,
Rosalind Lohrfinck
Secretary to Mr. Mencken

H. L. Mencken died January 29, 1956, at the house he was raised in at 1524 Hollins St., Baltimore. John Fante died from complications of diabetes on May 8, 1983, in the Motion Picture Hospital in Woodland Hills, California. Although the two men never met, Fante told an interviewer in 1979, "I would have done anything to get the praise of H. L. Mencken. I adored the guy."[85]

ENDNOTES

1. Carey McWilliams, *The Education of Carey McWilliams* (New York: Simon and Schuster, 1979), 55.

2. "Americana" was a feature that had its origins in *The Smart Set*, in which a state was mentioned followed by a newspaper piece or speech that pointed to the prejudices or stupidity of some of the state's inhabitants.

3. Mencken's *Treatise on the Gods* was published in March of 1930.

4. Anthony Comstock (1844–1915) was a self-appointed censor and often the butt of Mencken's sharp wit. Mencken is rejecting a story by Fante called "Charlie Bates." Comstock billed himself, on the title page of *Traps for the Young* (1883), as "Chief Special Agent of the New York Society for the Suppression of Vice," his own organization from which he fought numerous court battles over four decades to suppress literature and art he found offensive to his Puritan tastes. George Bernard Shaw popularized the word "comstockery" for the activities of Comstock and his followers after the censor sought to have the Irish playwright's *Mrs. Warren's Profession* banned from this country. This attempt failed, but he had a dangerously effective impact on American arts up through World War I and beyond (Broun: 17–18). In his *A Book of Prefaces* (253–59) Mencken attacks Comstock not just for having books banned — through passage of the Comstock bill attached to the Postal Act of 1873 — but also for enlisting a following of disciples who later were instrumental in initiating the follies of prohibition. By Mencken's account Comstock was directly responsible for having such works of literature outlawed as Thomas Hardy's *Jude the Obscure* and Harold Frederic's *The Damnation of Theron Ware*. Mencken fought the Comstocks in "The Hatrack" case in 1926, when Boston's Watch and Ward Society attempted to have *The Mercury* removed from the stands for publishing what they considered an obscene story, "The Hatrack." Mencken lost the court case on the

143

banning of the magazine from the mails on a technicality, but it was considered a battle won over comstockery (Bode: 270–75). In 1927, Mencken incurred the wrath of critics including Irving Babbitt for publishing the William Faulkner story, "The Evening Sun" (Manchester: 222).

5. In a letter to his mother, also dated July 26, Fante said: "I'm coming home. Leaving tomorrow, Wednesday. I'm forced to hitch-hike, consequently I don't know when I'll arrive. No need to worry, tho, for I'll make it somehow. Have promises of job in San Francisco." At the time, the family was reunited and living in Roseville, near Sacramento, California. Also in 1932, Fante made a trip to Denver, during which visit, according to friends Ross Wills and Carey McWilliams, he squandered money on old school friends and had to hitch-hike back to Los Angeles.

6. Ironically, although he never did become editor of *The American Mercury,* Fante did, in 1978, become blind from the effects of diabetes.

7. "Home Sweet Home" was published in *The American Mercury* in November of 1932.

8. Sherwood Anderson's short story, "I Want to Know Why," concerns an adolescent boy's confusion and curiosity about sex. He is puzzled and bewildered when he sees an older male he admires in the arms of a prostitute through the window of a brothel. Anderson (1876–1941), whom Fante mentions in several of the letters, is generally considered one of the best American fiction writers of the first half of the 20th Century. His most famous work is the collection of short stories, *Winesburg, Ohio.*

9. Gamaliel Bradford (1863–1932) and Lytton Strachey (1880–1932) were both biographers, the former American, the latter British. Among Bradford's works were *Damaged Souls, Darwin,* and *Bare Souls.* Strachey's main work was *Eminent Victorians.* Both are considered influential forebears of modern biography. It is hard to know what Fante is getting at here, unless his statement is in deference to Mencken's anti-British attitudes.

10. Both Friedrich Nietzsche and Richard Wagner were Germans whom Mencken greatly admired. He had earlier written the first biography of the philosopher in English entitled, *The Philosophy of Friedrich Nietzsche,* Boston: Luce, 1908.

11. Albert Halper (1904–1984) was a *Mercury* contributor and author of *Union Square* (1933), *The Foundry* (1934), *The Chute* (1937), *Sons of the Fathers* (1940) and *Good-bye Union Square* (1970), chiefly composed of working-class characters and based on his youth in Chicago.

12. The details of this story are unclear, but Julio Sal is the name Fante gave to a Filipino cannery worker in a Saturday Evening Post story published in 1941, "Helen, Thy Beauty Is to Me —." The story was later included in the anthology, *The Wine of Youth.* Fante's interest in the Filipinos derived from his early work with them in the canneries in Long Beach and Wilmington, California. He was later to use them in his stories and often thought of writing a longer work about the Filipino experience in California.

13. Charles Angoff (1902–1979) was assistant editor of the *Mercury* from 1925 to 1931, and later editor of the magazine. Although Mencken hired him, the Harvard-educated Angoff and he never got along, temperamentally. Perhaps Fante knew this. In Angoff's 1956 book, *H. L. Mencken: A Portrait from Memory,* he portrays his former boss as oafish and vulgar, possessing many prejudices and less than a first-rate intellect, an uncharacteristic assessment, which has since been attributed to Angoff's very different personal style from that of his former mentor.

14. Jim Tully (1888–1947), a frequent contributor to the *Mercury,* was a short story writer and novelist, who wrote largely autobiographical based works on his life as a hobo from the ages of 11 to 20. His *Beggars of Life* was published in 1926. He later became a publicist for Charlie Chaplin.

15. Guy J. Forgue, *Letters of H. L. Mencken.* Boston: Northeastern University Press, 1981. 352.

16. "First Communion" (which Mencken here calls "First Sacraments") was published in the *Mercury* in February of 1933.

17. Ellery Sedgwick was editor of *The Atlantic Monthly*.

18. *Making a President* was Mencken's account of the 1932 presidential conventions comprising dispatches that appeared in the *Baltimore Sun*, vividly depicting what the reporter perceived as the circus-like proceedings surrounding the Republican nomination of President Hoover and the Democratic battle between Al Smith and Franklin Roosevelt, where the latter emerged victorious. Mencken was a lifelong aficionado of the conventions, which he reported on up to 1948. In praising Mencken's book Fante quotes from Robert Browning's long poem, "The Ring and the Book" (in *The Complete Poetical Works of Browning*, Boston: Houghton Mifflin, 1895, p. 427). The original line is ". . . all a wonder and a wild desire." It is unclear why Fante cites the work.

19. Reference to "Big Leaguer," which appeared in the *Mercury* in March of 1933.

20. It is not clear why this seemingly innocuous letter is the only one which Mencken asks to be returned, but it is the only such letter in the correspondence.

21. *The American Mercury* sold for 50 cents a copy or $5 a year in 1933. A limited, all rag edition was sold for $1 a copy or $10 a year.

22. Fante, through an introduction by Mencken, was represented by Maxim Lieber, a top New York literary agent, who secured him the advance from Knopf for a book which was to have been called *Pater Doloroso*. They later parted company over Fante's failure to present Knopf with a workable manuscript. On May 27, 1936, Elizabeth Nowell, who then represented Fante, wrote, "He [Knopf] did it [paid the advance] because he had no American list and needed one, and because he had Mencken's say-so on you."

23. Fante did not save any writings that he couldn't use. No short stories exist except for those published by the *Mercury* and other magazines. It can't be determined what this particular story was or why Mencken rejected it.

24. Fante would have read the following AP report in the *Los Angeles Times* Saturday, October 7, 1933:

"Henry Hazlitt, former newspaperman and at present one of the editors of *The Nation*, will be the new editor of *The American Mercury*, from which position H. L. Mencken will retire at the end of the year.

"In confirming news of his retirement, Mencken said he wants to devote his time to writing books and to newspaper work."

25. Walter Lippmann (1889–1974) was a journalist and political commentator of great influence. He was founder of *The New Republic* magazine. Will Rogers (1879–1935) was a humorist, showman and political satirist who wrote newspaper columns and hosted radio programs throughout the 1920s and until his death in 1935.

26. Henry Hazlitt, a writer for *The Nation*, was picked by Mencken to succeed him as editor of the *Mercury*. Mencken chose Hazlitt because, unlike Angoff, he shared his conservative economic views. But Knopf soon became dissatisfied with Hazlitt and replaced him with Angoff. Fante did continue to publish in the *Mercury* through its various permutations over the years (it finally became a right-wing political organ with few respectable contributors), though he was later to refer to it as "a fascist rag" in an unpublished letter to Carey McWilliams.

27. Mencken published a series of six books of essays called *Prejudices* from 1919 to 1927.

28. *Babbitt*, by Sinclair Lewis, New York: Harcourt, Brace & World, 1922, 1950. A lampoon of the American middle class by one of Fante's favorite authors.

29. George Jean Nathan (1882–1958) founded *The Smart Set* with Mencken and was co-editor with Mencken of *The American Mercury* from 1924 to 1925. He founded *The American Spectator* in 1932, a literary and intellectual journal which directly competed with the *Mercury* for writers and readers. Among Nathan's books were *The Popular Theatre* (1918), *The Critic and the Drama* (1922), *Materia Critica* (1924), *The New American Credo* (1927), *Testament of a Critic* (1931) and *The Intimate Notebooks of George Jean Nathan* (1932). Many of his works, including the *Notebooks*, followed an epigrammatic style, as opposed to Mencken's broader strokes in the *Prejudices,* the former terse and clever, the latter, while none the less pointed and vivid, developing ideas with more detail.

30. The Long Beach earthquake of 1933, later depicted by Fante in *Ask the Dust* (1939; reprinted by Black Sparrow Press, 1980, 1987).

31. Fante lived with Helen Purcell in Long Beach. She was a music teacher, nine years his senior.

32. "My son Julius" is a clever sexual reference; Mencken never had a son.

33. The "Wirts" reference is obscure. Mencken published *Treatise on the Gods* in 1930 and *Treatise on Right and Wrong* in 1934. In the chapter of *Treatise on the Gods* entitled "Its State Today," included in the last 70 pages Fante refers to, Mencken reflects on the enlightened scientific thinking beginning with the Renaissance, which he called, "immensely curious, ingenious, skeptical and daring — in brief, everything that Christianity was not." He praises Galileo, Newton, Leibniz and other thinkers of the Renaissance and later. Of 18th century thought, he says that "Christian theology finally disappeared from the intellectual baggage of all really civilized men." (*Treatise on the Gods*, New York: Alfred A. Knopf, 1930. 174–75.) Fante apparently read the book with great delight.

34. James Branch Cabell (1879–1958) was a *Mercury* contributor and novelist whose books included *Jurgen* (1919), *Something About Eve* (1927) and *Let Me Lie* (1947), among many others.

35. David O. Selznick (1902–1965) was first a writer, then a film producer, whose credits included *A Star Is Born* (1937), *Gone With the Wind* (1939), *The Third Man* (1949) and many others. Fante is probably referring here to his collaborator on *Dinky* (1935), Frank Fenton. Fenton wrote such films as *Angel's Holiday* (1937), *The Sky's the Limit* (1943) and *The Jayhawkers* (1959). He received collaborative credits on many screenplays over three decades. In *Dreams From Bunker Hill* (1982), Fante based the character, Frank Edgington, on Fenton.

36. Maxim Lieber was an influential literary agent who took on Fante at Mencken's recommendation. He handled Fante from 1933 to 1936, placing several short stories for him and negotiating a contract for a novel with Alfred A. Knopf which never came to fruition. Fante's apparent animosity toward Lieber's rejection of a story was probably in reference to "A Bad Confession," about which Lieber said, in an unpublished letter dated July 25, 1934, "I'd also advise you against the bad habit of rewriting old stories. It is far better to write a new one. I say this apropos of 'A Bad Confession.' First of all you must know that you can't get away with certain phrases and actions, one of them being 'fornication.' " The story was never published. The reference to Lieber's Marxism is obscure. If Lieber was a Marxist there is no mention of it in extant letters between him and Fante.

37. In *The New Masses*, May 22, 1934, Hugh Cole wrote a review headlined "The Fool of Baltimore," which was an attack on *Treatise on Right and Wrong* and Mencken himself. In line with the magazine's Marxist slant, he said of Mencken's work, it "is not a work that issues any important challenge to the conventional ethics of a class society rank with falsity and meanness . . . it would be hard to imagine a book based on a more complete indifference to actual right and wrong, without capital letters, or on less real understanding of the forces that make for morality or immorality." He calls Mencken "one of the best amateur philologists in the country," faulting him for being out of his league when speaking of matters of morality and ethics.

38. In this letter Fante makes reference to the Longshoremen's strike against the Pacific Coast Shipowners on May 9, 1934. He also refers to Upton Sinclair's bid for the governorship of California on a platform known as "End Poverty in California" (EPIC). Sinclair (1878-1968) wrote a book at the time called *I, Governor of California and How I Ended Poverty*. Sinclair won the Democratic Party nomination for governor, but lost the general election to Republican Frank F. Merriam. Friedrich Nietzsche (1844-1900), a favorite of both Fante and Mencken, was insane for the last dozen years of his life.

39. The extremely influential William Cardinal O'Connell (1859-1944) of Boston was an outspoken advocate of moral restraint in films. He founded the Catholic Legion of Decency, which, by organized boycotts, effectively censored films and forced the industry to impose the Production Code of 1934, which became the moral arbiter of film content for the next three decades.

40. Mencken was a champion of German culture and traditions, in opposition to those of England. He publicly supported Germany in World War I and opposed our entry into the war, positions that didn't reckon well with his critics. William Manchester, in *Disturber of the Peace* (New York: Harper & Brothers, 1951:89-90), says of Mencken's *Baltimore Sun* essays in 1915, "he was a spokesman for Germany, and an arrogant and offensive spokesman at that." But after the United States entered the war Mencken's feelings became more ambivalent, and he remained publicly silent about the war.

41. Mencken never published *Advice to Young Men*. Mencken criticized social welfare programs in general and Roosevelt's New Deal in particular. President Roosevelt's Brain Trust was a group of policy advisers including Samuel Rosenman, Raymond Moley, Rexford Guy Tugwell, Adolf Berle, Jr. and Basil O'Connor.

42. Jackie Cooper (b. 1921) was a child actor who starred in *Dinky*, the Fante/Fenton collaboration, in 1935. He is now a

television director. Frankie Darro (1917–1976) was a character actor in films.

43. Joseph Breen (1890–1965) was in charge of RKO studios and later chairman of the Code and Rating Administration, popularly known as the Hays Office (for its first chairman, Will Hays) or the Breen Office, which was the film industry's self-censoring organization, founded in 1934 in response to claims by Cardinal O'Connell's Legion of Decency and others that films portrayed excessive sex and violence. The 1934 code was written by a Catholic priest, Father Daniel Lord, and a Catholic film distributor, Martin Quigley. Breen himself was a Catholic layman. The code, which imposed large fines on violators, controlled the content of films well into the 1950s. The self-censorship had virtually ended by the mid-1960s, when the new Motion Picture Code applied letter ratings to films.

44. Fante is probably referring to *Dinky*, the scenario for which he presented to Samuel Bischoff, the producer of the Warner Brothers project in 1935. Bischoff (1890–1975) was a notable producer whose credits include *The Charge of the Light Brigade* (1936), *You'll Never Get Rich* (1941), *Appointment in Berlin* (1943), *King of the Roaring Twenties* (1961) and *The Strangler* (1964).

45. Erskine Caldwell (b. 1903), besides working for a time in Hollywood, wrote *God's Little Acre* and *Tobacco Road,* and served as a foreign correspondent for *Life* magazine.

46. Tasker (1903–1944) and Booth (b. 1899) were prisoners whose writings were published by Mencken in the *Mercury*. Booth was serving a life sentence for bank robbery in California's Folsom prison when, in 1927, Alfred A. Knopf published his life story, *Stealing Through Life*. Knopf also published Tasker's prison book, *Grimhaven,* in 1927. Tasker was sequestered in San Quentin in California, also for armed robbery. Their crimes were apparently unrelated. Tasker, after release from prison, became a screenwriter, with credits including *A Notorious Gentleman* (1935), *Back Door to Heaven* (1939) and *Secrets of the Underground* (1942).

47. George Sterling (1869–1926), once a protégé of writer Ambrose Bierce, was a California poet and founder of the Carmel colony of artists and writers. Mencken refers to Sterling in *Heathen Days*, p. 187.

48. Ambrose Bierce (1842–c.1914) was a satirical and often caustic writer who served as a columnist for the *San Francisco Examiner* and disappeared in Mexico in 1913, while presumably covering the Mexican Revolution. Among his short stories, the most famous is "An Occurrence at Owl Creek Bridge." He also wrote *Fantastic Fables* and *The Devil's Dictionary*. Jack London (1876–1916) was one of California's most famous and prolific writers. Among his works are *Call of the Wild* (1903), *The Sea Wolf* (1904), *Martin Eden* (1906) and *John Barleycorn* (1913).

49. Dolores Del Rio (1905–1983) was a glamorous star of the 1930s and 1940s who acted in *Flying Down to Rio* (1932), *Madame Du Barry (1934), Journey Into Fear* (1942) and *The Fugitive* (1947), after which she returned to her native Mexico to act on stage and in films.

50. Kay Francis (1899–1968) was a star of the 1930s whose films included *A Notorious Affair* (1930), *Trouble in Paradise* (1933) and *Confession* (1937).

51. Barbara Stanwyck (b. 1907) was a film star of the 1930s and 1940s and is now primarily a television actress. She had roles in *Ever My Heart* (1933), *The Woman in Red* (1935), *Stella Dallas* (1937), *The Lady Eve* (1941) and *Double Indemnity* (1944).

52. Line from "Childe Harold's Pilgrimage," by Lord Byron, Canto IV, Stanza 179.

53. Erle Stanley Gardner (1889–1970) was most famous for his "Perry Mason" stories, which became film and, later, television dramas. Sir Hugh Walpole (1884–1941) was a New Zealand-born novelist who worked for a time in films. His books include *Jeremy* (1919) and *Portrait of a Man with Red Hair* (1925). While working as a scenarist in Hollywood, Walpole acted as the vicar in the film *David Copperfield* (1934).

54. Forgue: 378.

55. On its "March of Events" (Op-Ed) page for January 14, 1932, the *Los Angeles Examiner* ran a story by Mencken titled "Mr. Kipling." It was the story of a delivery man in Baltimore whom Mencken and his family called Mr. Kipling because of his bushy mustache and large, glittering eyeglasses. Fante may call it unusual for Mencken because, unlike much of his writings, it is neither bitingly critical nor at all cynical; it is a gentle story of a stoical old man who drove his horse-drawn cart through the neighborhood of Mencken's youth. Once stopping the cart at his family's gate and carrying in a large trunk on his back, Mencken recalls, "he was attacked with a horrible uproar by a new and saucy family dog," but, Mencken says, "he kept on up to our house without so much as a glance at the animal. Arrived at the kitchen door, he eased down his burden, took off his spectacles, mopped his face quietly, and contemplated the dog for the first time. 'When I come in,' he said calmly, 'it didn't hardly seem like he knowed me.' He mopped some more, and then added the serene corollary: 'But he won't not know me no more.' "

56. Joel Sayre (1901–1979) sat on the first board of the Screen Writers Guild in 1936. His screenplays included *Come On, Marines* (1934), *Annie Oakley* (1935) and *The Road to Glory* (1936), with William Faulkner, which Fante refers to in Letter 55.

57. After finishing her film acting career, Mary Pickford (1893–1979) wrote inspirational books including *Why Not Try God* (1934) and *The Demi-Widow* (1935).

58. Fante was living with a woman named Marie Baray, a model whom he once told his mother he was going to marry. She was, in part, the basis for Camilla in his 1939 novel, *Ask the Dust*.

59. Paul Palmer, a former associate of Mencken's at the *Baltimore Sun*, edited the *Mercury* after Hazlitt and Angoff. He published Fante's story, "Bricklayer in the Snow," in the issue of January, 1936.

60. Alfred A Knopf published Mencken's revised *American Language* in 1936.

61. Louis Adamic (1898–1951) wrote *My America, My Native Land* and *The Eagle and the Rock*, and was editor of *Common Ground* magazine.

62. Michael Gold (1893–1967) was one of the young writers of the 1930s helped along by Mencken, but in the September, 1931, issue of *The New Masses*, Gold demanded that Mencken retire from the *Mercury*, addressing his column to him with the exhortation, "You are a Tory who hates the Soviet Union. Worse that, you are a white Nordic chauvinist who fears and hates the yellow races." In a letter to writer James T. Farrell on December 11, 1940, Mencken said, "I never see Mike Gold's idiocies. The fact that he is denouncing me violently, however, doesn't surprise me. I gave him a hand in his early days. Such . . . always prove their independence of spirit by libeling those who have tried to help them. Mike had a certain mild talent, but politics, of course, ruined it. When the pogroms start in this great Republic he will probably be one of the first victims."

63. William Soskin (1889–1952) was a literary critic who became executive editor of the publishers Stackpole Sons. He was responsible for the publication of Fante's novels, *Wait Until Spring, Bandini* (1938) and *Ask the Dust* (1939). In later years, Soskin was editor for the Book-of-the-Month Club.

64. Father Charles Edward Coughlin (1891–1980) was the "radio priest" for a 47-station network run out of his offices at the Shrine of the Little Flower in Chicago. When his popular broadcasts started in 1930, Coughlin presented a populist image, denouncing the exploitation of the poor by bankers and entrepreneurs, and supporting Roosevelt's 1932 campaign for the presidency, but his proclamations turned to demagoguery and racism. His broadcasts and publication of a paper, *Social Justice*, continued to 1942, with attacks against Roosevelt and the Jews and other ethnic minorities. His listeners were once thought to number 30 to 40 million, but diminished as his message became

increasingly vituperative. There was evidence that Coughlin received financial backing and broadcast copy from Nazi Germany. He was closely identified with the German-American Bund, and his followers were among the ranks of those arrested for acts of violence against Jewish store owners in and around New York City during the late 1930s. ("The Radio Priest and His Flock," by Wallace Stegner in *The Aspirin Age,* ed. Isabel Leighton, New York: Simon and Schuster, 1949.)

65. Alexander Kerensky (1881–1970) was a member of the liberal provisional government of Russia following the reign of the Romanovs. He was a moderate socialist who left Russia after Lenin took charge. He was later a professor at Stanford University in California.

66. Although the reference is obscure, if Sayre did flee to Mexico, as Fante suggests, he returned to continue to work in Hollywood.

67. Fante refers to scenarists John Bright and Nat West. Nathanael West (1903–1940) is highly regarded for his works of fiction, particularly *Day of the Locust* and *Miss Lonelyhearts.* In his biography *Nathanael West: The Art of His Life,* Jay Martin says of the writer that although he disdained taking a partisan stand in the politics of the day, he agreed to make a speech at the conference supporting the writers' right to organize as a union. John Bright (b. 1908) wrote *Blonde Crazy* (1931), *The Public Enemy* (1931), *She Done Him Wrong* (1933) and others. He was later to flee to Mexico to avoid a subpoena by the House Un-American Activities Committee. He now continues to work in Hollywood.

68. Ella Winter (1898–1980) was a writer and the wife of the journalist and social critic Lincoln Steffens (1866–1936). Winter wrote *Red Virtue: Human Relationships in the New Russia* (1933) and edited the *Letters of Lincoln Steffens* (1938). Steffens' most enduring work is his *Autobiography* (1931). Steffens was known as a skeptic and as the father of muckraking journalism. Fante here may be questioning how the great muckraker could have been matched with Winter, a rather doctrinaire Stalinist as evidenced

by her apologia for the Soviet regime, *Red Virtue*. But Steffens himself was a supporter of Russian communism.

69. Charles Erskine Scott Wood (1852–1944) was an army officer and lawyer who turned to writing in later life. His books include *The Poet in the Desert* (1915) and *Heavenly Discourse* (1927).

70. Dorothy Parker (1893–1967) was a journalist and short story writer. She was on the staff of *Vogue* and *Vanity Fair* and later wrote for the *New Yorker*.

71. Harry Bridges (b. 1900) was born in Australia. He immigrated to the United States in the early 1930s, joining the International Longshoreman's and Warehouseman's Union in 1937. He served as the union's president for nearly four decades, maintaining a reputation as one of California's most influential and controversial labor leaders, and an avowed Marxist.

72. Mencken never published *Advice to Young Men*.

73. Mencken's error for Roseville.

74. O. Henry, *The Complete Works of O. Henry*, ed. Harry Hansen (Garden City: Doubleday & Company, 1953), vii.

75. Mencken's editorial in the March 4, 1938, edition of the *Baltimore Sun* was entitled "Five Years of the New Deal." The lengthy piece was a diatribe against the economic and social programs of the Roosevelt administration which Mencken found wasteful and unproductive, and concluded with the observation that "The one genuine beneficiary of all the roar of words, and storm of lawmaking, and looting of savings, and multiplicity of jobholders has been the least deserving of all American citizens — the one-crop farmer with nothing in his head and too many children and hookworms; the city proletarian with a bad trade, or half a good one, or no trade at all; the chronic and incurable incompetent, bemused all his days by envy of his betters. Here is the real pet of the New Deal, and the keystone of its singularly idiotic moral theology." It is difficult to speculate on what Fante

156

identified with in the article. He apparently didn't share Mencken's disdain for Roosevelt's leadership of the country through the Depression, later telling him that he intended to vote for him in 1940.

76. Willard Huntington Wright (1888–1939) was a newspaper critic and editor of *The Smart Set* prior to Mencken. He wrote *What Nietzsche Taught* (1914), and went on to publish, under the pseudonym S. S. Van Dine, a number of popular mystery stories including *The Bishop Murder Case* (1929), *The Dragon Murder Case* (1933) and the *Philo Vance Murder Cases* (1936).

77. Mencken had written *The Philosophy of Friedrich Nietzsche* in 1908. In a letter to Edward Stone dated March 1, 1937, he said, "My knowledge of Nietzsche at that time was very superficial. Most of his books had not been translated. I tackled the original German and found it dreadful going. However, after a winter of hard work, I managed to formulate a more or less coherent idea of his system, and upon that basis I wrote my book. It made unexpected success, and is still in print. It should have been revised long ago, but Schaff for some reason or other refuses to let me touch it."

78. Fante is referring to print and radio journalists of the time. Hans Von (H.V.) Kaltenborn (1878–1965) was a newspaperman and radio commentator who reported on the war in Europe from 1940 on. He was pro-British, as the whole country soon would be, in opposition to Hitler. Elmer Davis (1890–1958) was a reporter and news analyst for CBS radio. John Gunther (1901–1970) was a foreign news correspondent who covered many important world events for nearly half a century. For NBC, he covered the outbreak of war in London in 1939. He later authored several books about his experiences. Raymond Swing (1887–1968), also a radio commentator, worked for the BBC during the war years. Wythe Williams (1881–1956) covered both World War I and II, and was political commentator for WOR-Mutual Broadcasting System from 1940 to 1941.

79. Although John Fante was a staunch liberal all of his adult life, this letter reflects an isolationist and anti-British attitude in the United States that had numerous adherents as President Roosevelt moved the country closer to involvement in World War II. Although World War I still held fearful memories for most Americans, it was primarly conservative Republicans in Congress who advocated isolation in 1940. But it was Wendell Willkie, who shared Roosevelt's opinion that we had to help our allies to defend ourselves, who won the 1940 Republican nomination, severely diminishing the isolationist position. Mencken opposed United States entry into World War I, and maintained similar views against entering into a new war in Europe. He was opposed to entry into World War I (see note No. 40, above) for two reasons: firstly, he had a cultural and philosophical affinity toward Germany and, secondly, he was opposed to war on principle. During the mid-1930s, Mencken got himself into trouble with *The American Mercury* publisher, Alfred A. Knopf, as well as with editors at the *Baltimore Sun* for underplaying the threat posed by Adolf Hitler (see "Hitlerismus," *The American Mercury*, December, 1933). In the above letter, Fante lampoons both President Roosevelt and the pro-war advocates.

80. Fante did produce five or six chapters of a novel on the Filipino experience in California for Pascal Covici of Viking Press, but Covici rejected the novel and Fante abandoned the project.

81. Irvin Cobb (1876–1944) was a newspaper reporter, short story writer, radio personality and film writer and actor.

82. Frank Sullivan (1892–1976) was first a newspaperman, then a fiction writer. His humorous books include *In One Ear* (1933), *A Pearl in Every Oyster* and *A Moose in the Hoose* (1959). He was a contributor to the *New Yorker* magazine. James Thurber (1894–1961), also a longtime contributor to the *New Yorker,* wrote humorous stories and drew cartoons. Among his books are *My Life and Hard Times* (1934), *The Thurber Carnival* (1935) and *Fables for Our Time* (1941).

83. Fante had long hoped to gain a Guggenheim Fellowship. In a 1934 letter to his mother he talked of getting the grant to live and write in Italy for a year. On November 27, 1940, Mencken wrote to Henry Allen Moe at the Guggenheim Foundation: "I am enclosing your questionnaire, with my notes. Haven't you an application from John Fante of California? He wrote to me some time ago that he was asking for a fellowship. If he does so, I recommend him. Indeed, he is a more likely young man than any of those on the enclosed sheet, save only [Henry] Miller." (From Mencken's letters in the New York Public Library.)

84. Stanley Kramer (b. 1913) produced such films as *Death of a Salesman* (1951), *High Noon* (1952), *On the Beach* (1959) and *Inherit the Wind* (1960). *Full of Life* was published by Little, Brown in 1952. Fante was later assigned to write the screenplay for the film which was produced in 1956, starring Judy Holliday and Richard Conte. It was to be the screenplay and film he would finally be most proud of.

85. From an unpublished interview with Ben Pleasants, May 29, 1979.

FANTE AND MENCKEN:
A SELECTED BIBLIOGRAPHY

WORKS BY JOHN FANTE

SHORT STORIES:

"Altar Boy," *The American Mercury,* August, 1932.
"Home Sweet Home," *The American Mercury,* November, 1932.
"First Communion," *The American Mercury,* March, 1933.
"Big Leaguer," *The American Mercury,* March, 1933.
"Odyssey of a Wop," *The American Mercury,* September, 1933.
"One of Us," *The Atlantic Monthly,* October, 1934.
"Washed in the Rain," *Westways,* October, 1934.
"Bricklayer in the Snow," *The American Mercury,* January, 1936.
"A Kidnaping in the Family," *Harper's Bazaar,* June, 1936.
"We Snatch a Frail," *The Pacific Weekly,* November, 1936 (with
    Frank Fenton).
"Postman Rings and Rings," *The American Mercury,* March, 1937.
"Charge It," *Scribner's Magazine,* April, 1937.
"The Road to Hell," *The American Mercury,* October, 1937.
"None So Blind," *Woman's Home Companion,* April, 1938.
"A Nun No More," *Virginia Quarterly Review,* October, 1940.
"Helen, Thy Beauty Is to Me," *The Saturday Evening Post,* March,
    1941.
"The Taming of Valenti," *Esquire,* April, 1941.

"That Wonderful Bird," *Good Housekeeping,* May, 1941.
"Mary Osaka, I Love You," *Good Housekeeping,* October, 1942.
"The Scoundrel," *Woman's Home Companion,* March, 1945.
"Papa Christmas Tree," *Woman's Home Companion,* December, 1946.
"The Dreamer," *Woman's Home Companion,* June, 1947.
"Wine of Youth," *Woman's Home Companion,* December, 1948.
"One Play Oscar," *The Saturday Evening Post,* November, 1950.
"In the Spring," *Collier's,* March, 1952.
"Full of Life" (excerpt), *Reader's Digest,* May, 1952.
"Big Hunger," *Collier's,* August, 1952.
"My Father's God," *Italian Americana,* Autumn, 1975.

ARTICLES:

"Bill Saroyan," *Common Ground,* Winter, 1941.

SCREENPLAYS:

Dinky (with Frank Fenton), Warner Brothers, 1935.
East of the River (with Ross Wills), Warner Brothers, 1940.
The Golden Fleecing, Metro-Goldwyn-Mayer, 1940.
Youth Runs Wild, RKO, 1944.
My Man and I, MGM, 1952.
Full of Life, Columbia Pictures, 1956.
Jeanne Eagels, Columbia Pictures, 1957.
Walk on the Wild Side (with Edmund Morris), Columbia Pictures, 1962.
The Reluctant Saint, Dmytryk-Weiler, 1962.
My Six Loves, Paramount, 1963.
Maya, MGM, 1966.

TELEVISION PLAY:

Something for a Lonely Man, Universal Television, 1967.

BOOKS:

Wait Until Spring, Bandini, New York: Stackpole, 1938; Santa
   Barbara: Black Sparrow Press, 1983.
Ask the Dust, New York: Stackpole, 1939; Santa Barbara: Black
   Sparrow Press, 1980.
Dago Red, New York: Viking Press, 1940. [contents reprinted
   as part of *The Wine of Youth,* 1985]
Full of Life, Boston: Little, Brown and Co., 1952; Santa Rosa:
   Black Sparrow Press, 1987.
The Brotherhood of the Grape, Boston: Houghton Mifflin Co., 1977;
   Santa Rosa: Black Sparrow Press, 1988.
Dreams From Bunker Hill, Santa Barbara: Black Sparrow Press,
   1982.
1933 Was a Bad Year, Santa Barbara: Black Sparrow Press, 1985.
The Road to Los Angeles, Santa Barbara: Black Sparrow Press,
   1985.
The Wine of Youth, Santa Barbara: Black Sparrow Press, 1985.
West of Rome, Santa Rosa: Black Sparrow Press, 1986.

WORKS BY H. L. MENCKEN

MAGAZINE ARTICLES:

"The National Literature," *Yale Review,* July, 1920.
"The Motive of the Critic," *The New Republic,* October 26, 1921.
"American Puritanism at Bay," *The Outlook* (London), February
   11, 1922.
"Three Years of Prohibition in America," *The Outlook,* June,
   1922.
"Joseph Conrad," *The Nation,* August 20, 1924.
"On Living in the United States," *The Nation,* December 7, 1926.
"What I Believe," *Forum,* September, 1930.
"Future of English," *Harper's Magazine,* April, 1935.

"The American Language," *Yale Review,* March, 1936.

"The New Deal Mentality," *The American Mercury,* May, 1936.

"The American Future," *The American Mercury,* February, 1937.

"That Was New York. The Life of an Artist (Theodore Dreiser)," *The New Yorker,* April 17, 1948.

"My Current Reading," *Saturday Review of Literature,* May 22, 1948.

"Some Opprobrious Nicknames," *American Speech,* February, 1949.

BOOKS:

The Philosophy of Friedrich Nietzsche. Boston: Luce, 1908; London: Fisher Unwin, 1908.

A Book of Burlesques. New York: Lane, 1916; London: Jonathan Cape, 1923.

A Book of Prefaces. New York: Knopf, 1917; London: Jonathan Cape, 1922.

In Defense of Women. New York: Philip Goodman, 1918; London: Jonathan Cape, 1923.

The American Language. New York: Knopf, 1919, 1921, 1923 and 1936 (four editions, each subsequent volume revised and expanded by Mencken). *Supplement I* and *Supplement II* published in 1945 and 1948, also by Knopf.

Prejudices: First Series. New York: Knopf, 1919; London: Jonathan Cape, 1921.

Prejudices: Second Series. New York: Knopf, 1920; London: Jonathan Cape, 1921.

Prejudices: Third Series. New York: Knopf, 1922; London: Jonathan Cape, 1923.

Prejudices: Fourth Series. New York: Knopf, 1924; London: Jonathan Cape, 1925.

Notes on Democracy. New York: Knopf, 1926; London: Jonathan Cape, 1927.

Prejudices: Fifth Series. New York: Knopf, 1926; London: Jonathan Cape, 1927.

Prejudices: Sixth Series. New York: Knopf, 1927; London: Jonathan Cape, 1928.

Treatise on the Gods. New York and London: Knopf, 1930; second edition: Knopf, 1946.

Making a President. New York: Knopf, 1932.

Treatise on Right and Wrong. New York: Knopf, 1934; London: Kegan Paul, Trench, Trubner, 1934; Toronto: The Ryerson Press, 1934.

Happy Days, 1880-1892. New York: Knopf, 1940; London: Kegan Paul, Trench, Trubner, 1940; Toronto: The Ryerson Press, 1942.

Newspaper Days, 1899-1906. New York: Knopf, 1941; London: Kegan Paul, Trench, Trubner, 1942; Toronto: The Ryerson Press, 1942.

Heathen Days, 1890-1936. New York: Knopf, 1943; Toronto: The Ryerson Press, 1943.

Christmas Story. New York: Knopf, 1946; Toronto: The Ryerson Press, 1946.

A Mencken Chrestomathy. New York: Knopf, 1949.

Mencken's Last Campaign: H. L. Mencken on the 1948 Election. Ed. Joseph C. Goulden. Washington, D.C.: The New Republic Book Company, 1976.

ADDITIONAL SOURCES FOR THIS VOLUME

Aaronson, Charles S., ed. *International Motion Picture Almanac.* New York: Quigley Publications, 1970.

Allen, Frederick Lewis. *Only Yesterday: An Informal History of the Nineteen-Twenties.* New York: Harper & Row, 1931.

Angoff, Charles. *H. L. Mencken: A Portrait from Memory.* New York: Thomas Yoseloff, 1956.

Bode, Carl. *Mencken.* Carbondale: Southern Illinois University Press, 1969.

Bode, Carl, ed. *The New Mencken Letters.* New York: The Dial Press, 1977.

Booth, Ernest. *Stealing Through Life.* New York: Alfred A. Knopf, 1927.

Bordman, Gerald. *The Oxford Companion to American Theatre*. New York, Oxford: Oxford University Press, 1984.

Broun, Heywood and Margaret Leech. *Anthony Comstock: Roundsman of the Lord*. New York: The Literary Guild of America, 1927.

Brown, Gene, ed. *The New York Times Encyclopedia of Film: 1896-1979*. New York: New York Times Books, 1984.

Comstock, Anthony. *Traps for the Young*. New York: Funk and Wagnalls, 1883.

Cooke, Alistair. "H. L. Mencken: The Public and the Private Face," in *Six Men*. New York: Knopf, 1977.

Dimmitt, Richard Bertrand. *A Title Guide to the Talkies*. New York: The Scarecrow Press, 1965.

Forgue, Guy J., ed. *Letters of H. L. Mencken*. Boston: Northeastern University Press, 1981.

Fecher, Charles A. *Mencken: A Study of His Thought*. New York: Knopf, 1978.

Feis, Herbert. *1933: Characters in Crisis*. Boston: Little, Brown, 1966.

Friedrich, Otto. *City of Nets: A Portrait of Hollywood in the 1940's*. New York: Harper & Row, 1986.

Garraty, John A. *The Great Depression*. New York: Harcourt Brace Jovanovich, 1986.

Goldston, Robert. *The Great Depression: The United States in the Thirties*. New York: Ballantine, 1984.

Halliwell, Leslie. *The Filmgoer's Companion*. New York: Hill & Wang, 1977.

Harvey, Sir Paul, ed. *The Oxford Companion to English Literature*. Oxford: Oxford University Press, 1985.

Hemingway, Ernest. *The Sun Also Rises*. New York: Charles Scribner's Sons, 1926.

Henry, O. *The Complete Works of O. Henry*. Ed. Harry Hansen. New York: Doubleday & Company, 1953.

Knopf, Alfred A. "H. L. Mencken: A Memoir," in Dorsey, John, ed., *On Mencken*. New York: Knopf, 1980.

Kurian, George. *Dictionary of Biography*. New York: Dell, 1980.

Langman, Larry. *A Guide to American Screenwriters*. New York: Garland, 1984.

Leighton, Isabel. *The Aspirin Age: 1919–1941.* New York: Simon & Schuster, 1949.

Leuchtenburg, William E. *Franklin D. Roosevelt and the New Deal: 1932–1940.* New York: Harper & Row, 1963.

Leuchtenburg, William E., ed. *The New Deal: A Documentary History.* New York: Harper & Row, 1968.

Louchheim, Katie, ed. *The Making of the New Deal: The Insiders Speak.* Cambridge: Harvard University Press, 1983.

McElveen, J. James. "H. L. Mencken," in Ashley, Perry J., ed., *Dictionary of Literary Biography: American Newspaper Journalists, 1926–1950* (v. 29). Detroit: Bruccoli Clark, 1984.

McWilliams, Carey. *Southern California Country: An Island on the Land.* New York: Duell, Sloan & Pearce, 1946.

McWilliams, Carey. *The Education of Carey McWilliams.* New York: Simon & Schuster, 1978.

Magill, Frank N., ed. *Cyclopedia of World Authors.* Englewood Cliffs, N.J.: Salem Press, 1974.

Manchester, William. *Disturber of the Peace: The Life of H. L. Mencken.* New York: Harper & Brothers, 1951.

Martin, Jay. *Nathanael West: The Art of His Life.* New York: Farrar, Straus and Giroux, 1970.

Mast, Gerald. *A Short History of the Movies.* New York: Bobbs-Merrill, 1971.

Morison, Samuel Eliot. *The Oxford History of the American People.* New York: New American Library, 1965.

Nolte, William H. *The Merrill Checklist of H. L. Mencken.* Columbus: Charles E. Merrill, 1969.

Olson, James S., ed. *Historical Dictionary of the New Deal.* Westport, Conn.: Greenwood Press, 1985.

Paneth, Donald. *The Encyclopedia of American Journalism.* New York: Facts on File Publications, 1983.

Rodgers, Marion Elizabeth, ed. *Mencken & Sara: A Life in Letters.* New York: McGraw-Hill, 1987.

Rolle, Andrew F. *California: A History.* Arlington Heights, Ill.: AHM, 1978.

Rolle, Andrew F. *Los Angeles: From Pueblo to City of the Future.* San Francisco: Boyd & Fraser, 1981.

Rosten, Leo. *Hollywood: The Movie Colony; The Movie Makers.* New York: Harcourt, Brace, 1941.

Singleton, M. K. *H. L. Mencken and the American Mercury Adventure*. Durham, N.C.: Duke University Press, 1962.

Schwartz, Nancy Lynn. *The Hollywood Writers' Wars*. New York: Knopf, 1982.

Tasker, Robert Joyce. *Grimhaven*. New York: Alfred A. Knopf, 1927.

Webster's Biographical Dictionary. Springfield, Mass.: G. & C. Merriam, 1974.

Who Was Who in America: With Notables. Chicago: Marquis Who's Who.

INDEX

170

171

Printed June 1989 in Santa Barbara & Ann
Arbor for the Black Sparrow Press by Graham
Mackintosh & Edwards Brothers, Inc. Design by
Barbara Martin. This edition is published in
paper wrappers; there are 750 hardcover trade
copies; & 176 numbered deluxe copies have
been handbound in boards by Earle Gray.

JOHN FANTE was born in Colorado in 1909. He attended parochial school in Boulder, and Regis High School, a Jesuit boarding school. He also attended the University of Colorado and Long Beach Junior College.

Fante began writing in 1929 and published his first short story in *The American Mercury* in 1932. He published numerous short stories in *The Atlantic Monthly, The American Mercury, The Saturday Evening Post, Collier's, Esquire,* and *Harper's Bazaar.* His first novel, *Wait Until Spring, Bandini,* was published in 1938. The following year *Ask the Dust* appeared. (Both novels have been reprinted by Black Sparrow Press.) In 1940 a collection of his short stories, *Dago Red,* was published.

Meanwhile, Fante had been occupied extensively in screenwriting. Some of his credits include *Full of Life, Jeanne Eagels, My Man and I, The Reluctant Saint, Something for a Lonely Man, My Six Loves* and *Walk on the Wild Side.*

John Fante was stricken with diabetes in 1955 and its complications brought about blindness in 1978, but he continued to write by dictation to his wife, Joyce, and the result was *Dreams from Bunker Hill* (Black Sparrow Press, 1982). He died at the age of 74 on May 8, 1983.

In 1985 Black Sparrow published Fante's selected stories, *The Wine of Youth,* and two early novels, which had never before been published, *The Road to Los Angeles* and *1933 Was a Bad Year.* In 1986 Black Sparrow brought out two previously unpublished novellas under the title *West of Rome. Full of Life* and *The Brotherhood of the Grape* were reprinted by Black Sparrow in 1988.

HENRY LOUIS MENCKEN was born in Baltimore, Maryland, on September 12, 1880, the first child of August and Anna Abhau Mencken, themselves children of German immigrants who prospered in the transported German culture of the Southeastern seaport.

When he was three years old the family, which was later to include Mencken's younger siblings, Charles, Gertrude and August, moved to 1524 Hollins Street, where H. L. Mencken was to live the rest of his life, except for his five years of marriage to Sara Haardt, from 1930 to 1935.

His father ran a prospering cigar factory in Baltimore, which he fully intended Mencken to take over from him, vehemently opposing the younger man's interest in writing and journalism, interests that were probably forged in the family's own library, where the young Henry discovered such writers as Mark Twain. He was later to say that reading *Huckleberry Finn* was "probably the most stupendous event of my whole life."

After graduating at the top of his class at the age of 16 from the Baltimore Polytechnic Institute he worked for a time at his father's factory, but was later to say he got nothing from the experience but a taste for cigars.

At 18, he went to work for the *Baltimore Morning Herald,* where he worked as a messenger, police reporter and editor before he moved, in 1906, to the *Baltimore Sun,* beginning a relationship as reporter, editor and columnist that was to last, with a few interruptions, for the rest of his life.

Over the next five decades, through sheer output of work, and editorship of the *Sun,* as well as two prestigious magazines, *The Smart Set* and *The American Mercury,* Mencken became the most powerful journalist in America. And because of his iconoclasm and devastating wit he became the ideal to which journalists and writers of prose aspired. Through his literary criticism and publishing of promising writers he promoted such eminent American authors as Sherwood Anderson, Theodore Dreiser and John Fante.

While never long abandoning his primary role as a journalist, he managed over his long career to produce a trilogy of memoirs, *Happy Days* (1940), *Newspaper Days* (1941) and *Heathen Days* (1943); several books of essays and critical pieces, and the still revered philological volume, *The American Language* (1918).

In 1930 he married a young devotee, Sara Haardt Mencken, 20 years his junior, who died five years later of tuberculosis. They had no children, and he was never again to marry.

Soon after reporting on the 1948 Presidential conventions, Mencken suffered a stroke, which left him incapacitated for the remainder of his life. He died in his sleep at the family home on Hollins Street on January 29, 1956.